"In *Perfectly Hidden Depression*, Margaret Rutherford shines a powerful and revealing spotlight on an important aspect of depression that receives far too little attention. As she describes in exquisite detail, the relationship between perfectionism and depression is an intense one; it creates a toxic internal environment that robs worthy people of the ability to enjoy even true successes, since perfection rarely, if ever, exists in the real world. Rutherford's compassion and wisdom is matched by her courage in challenging all of us to expand our understanding of depression in its diverse appearances. The guidance and support she provides here will be invaluable for anyone struggling with these debilitating issues."

—**Michael D. Yapko, PhD**, clinical psychologist, and author of *Depression Is Contagious* and *Keys to Unlocking Depression*

"*Perfectly Hidden Depression* illustrates a critical truth that we need to face: sometimes, the people who appear to have it all together are falling apart. Margaret Rutherford shows us that hiding depression through perfectionism can be deadly. This book shows you how to recognize depression in yourself, overcome the stigma, shed unhealthy perfectionism, and embrace your imperfect self."

—**Sarah Fader**, CEO of Stigma Fighters, and coauthor of *The 10-Step Depression Relief Workbook*

"Margaret Rutherford's book, *Perfectly Hidden Depression*, is a unique perspective on a common, but often unrecognized, cause of depression. People who experience this version of depression almost always seem fine on the outside, and give little, if any, signs of their inner suffering…. Driven by perfectionism, unrealistic demands on themselves, and harsh internal self-criticism and shame, they often suffer this hidden form of depression. They feel stuck in an inexplicable trap of depression, and do not know how to change and heal this.

This book is exceptionally written. It clearly describes this condition and maps out concrete strategies for confronting these problems. Aside from many realistic strategies for confronting hidden depression is a core feature of developing more self-compassion and recognizing one's vulnerability…. I highly recommend this amazing book to those who suffer from depression, the significant others in their lives, as well as psychotherapists."

—**John Preston, PsyD**, therapist, author, and professor
emeritus at the California School of Professional
Psychology and Alliant International University

"This book can and will save lives. Written with wisdom and compassion, *Perfectly Hidden Depression* not only sheds light on a growing epidemic, but provides a clear path for coming out of hiding into healing."

—**Pat Love, EdD**, licensed marriage and family therapist,
and author of *The Truth About Love*

"Finally, a book that takes a deep dive into what psychologists have called 'masked depression,' but has no diagnostic label. If you are a self-critical perfectionist, and are suffering in silence, this book offers a pathway to getting the help you need. If you know you are in pain but didn't have the words to ask for help and connect with others, Margaret Robinson Rutherford's book will offer you a new beginning. You can look forward to transformational self-insights that will help you move from shame to self-compassion."

—**Lara Honos-Webb, PhD**, worldwide attention deficit disorder (ADD) expert; clinical psychologist; and author of *The Gift of ADHD*, *The Gift of ADHD Activity Book*, *The Gift of Adult ADD*, *The ADHD Workbook for Teens*, and *Listening to Depression*

"For anyone who feels like they don't 'deserve' the label of depression, or for anyone who finds themselves silently stuck in cycles of self-hate, Margaret Rutherford's work on perfectly hidden depression strikes in a place most literature on depression misses, speaking to a whole group of people who suffer without acknowledging or feeling worthy of their own pain. I recognized myself in these pages, and wish a younger version of myself had been introduced to this book and the helpful reflection prompts within it. I hope it reaches the people who need it."

—**Sarah Schuster**, editorial director of contributors at *The Mighty*

# Perfectly Hidden Depression

How to Break Free
from the **Perfectionism** That
Masks Your Depression

MARGARET ROBINSON RUTHERFORD, PhD

New Harbinger Publications, Inc.

## Publisher's Note

Distributed in Canada by Raincoast Books

New Harbinger Publications, Inc.
5674 Shattuck Avenue
Oakland, CA 94609
www.newharbinger.com

Cover design by Amy Shoup

Acquired by Jennye Garibaldi

Edited by Jennifer Holder and Marisa Solís

Library of Congress Cataloging-in-Publication Data on file

Printed in the United States of America

21    20    19

10    9    8    7    6    5    4    3    2    1        First Printing

*To my husband, Richard. It's my turn to do the laundry.*

# Contents

## PART I:
### Understanding Perfectly Hidden Depression

## PART II:
### The Five Stages of Healing
#### Consciousness, Commitment, Confrontation, Connection, Change

# Foreword

I first learned about the term "perfectly hidden depression" when I read a Facebook update posted by Dr. Margaret Rutherford. What she wrote there prompted me to visit her blog, where I viewed a video with even more incredibly eye-opening details.

*This makes so much sense,* I thought to myself. *People experiencing perfectly hidden depression hide behind a mask of perfection, but inside they are suffering deeply.*

And in the same breath I found myself wondering, *But why does it have to be so hard for them to share their struggles? If they're in so much pain, wouldn't they naturally be driven to ask for help?*

Several years ago a family in my community tragically lost their teenage son to suicide. Jay was the person anyone would label a model student. Smart, funny, athletic, well liked among his peers, and motivated—always aspiring to succeed, never wanting to fail.

But behind the mask of perfection, this talented young man in my town was hurting. No one would have ever guessed by observing Jay from the outside that, on the inside, his world was drastically different. He was suffering intensely. He felt that there was no way he'd ever find relief from the pain—so much so that he decided to leave this world.

I met Jay's mom, Erin, when she purchased Brave Bead bracelets from my organization, This Is My Brave, for Jay's surviving sisters. Erin was encouraged by the work we're doing to break down the stigma surrounding mental illness that prevents many from seeking help. Our organization provides a platform for individuals to tell their true, personal stories about mental health issues and addiction onstage through creative expression. Those in the audience are filled with hope as they watch someone stand up in front of strangers to talk about their journey, from their darkest lows to how they found recovery to how they're now thriving. It's our goal to shift the perspective from a place of fear and avoidance to one of hope and acceptance. We do this through sharing stories.

Dr. Margaret's book shares the same goal by shining a light on a critically important subject that is silently screaming to be better understood: perfectly hidden depression. Mental health problems, and specifically the suicide epidemic, have become a major public health crisis.

This book is for everyone because, whether we realize it or not, we are all touched by mental health issues. One in five Americans (46.6 million, or 18.5 percent of the population) experiences a mental health condition in a given year (National Institute of Mental Health 2019b). Since we all know more than five people in our lives, we *all* know someone touched by a mental illness—and that someone could be ourselves.

In the United States, 17.3 million adults experience a major depressive episode in a year (National Institute of Mental Health 2019a), and suicide is currently the second leading cause of death among those ages ten to thirty-four (National Institute of Mental Health 2018). *Perfectly Hidden Depression* is not only an incredible resource for individuals caught in the grips of this syndrome, but it's also an insightful tool for anyone seeking to better understand depression and anxiety in general, and how these conditions manifest in various ways in different people.

I truly believe that the only way we as a society are going to end the stigma and fear surrounding mental illness is by putting our names and faces on our stories. This means finding the courage to be brave and remove the masks we've created to shield our vulnerabilities from the world. Realizing that our vulnerabilities are also what have made us into the complex, unique, beautiful human beings we are is the starting point to a more rich, fulfilling, connected life.

I didn't have the opportunity to meet Jay before he died, but it's my feeling that had he and his family known what Dr. Margaret explains in her book, he could've had a solid chance at surviving his depression. It absolutely breaks my heart that they didn't have the wealth of knowledge you're about to read. *Perfectly Hidden Depression* contains the stepping-stones to walk away from the isolating, painful grip of perfectionism and embrace self-love and acceptance.

You're about to embark on a powerful journey, and I can't wait for you to get started.

—Jennifer Marshall
Executive director and cofounder
This Is My Brave, Inc.
https://thisismybrave.org

# Preface

I'm a psychologist. Occasionally I receive an emergency call, usually from someone who's feeling overwhelmed.

On a beautiful fall day in 1998, my pager went off just before noon. It was Rick, Natalie's husband.

"I'm really worried about her," he said, "but I'm out of town and won't be back for three or four more hours."

Natalie had been in therapy for anxiety, as she felt out of control trying to handle work and kids. She hated her overly busy life but felt intense guilt about admitting it. She struggled with a constant need to please, although she never felt as if she did enough. Natalie spoke apologetically, as if focusing on her problems was unseemly or self-centered. She told me, "I shouldn't complain. I have it easy compared with most people."

Her laugh, when I heard it, was nervous and forced, but there was always a smile on her face, even when she was talking about something painful. As of late, Natalie had been drinking more—"only when the kids are in bed"—to take the edge off.

"I think she's at home," Rick said over the phone. "She took the kids to school, and it's her day off. I called, but she's not answering. Last time I talked to her, she sounded weird. She asked me to pick up the kids. Has she said anything to you about being down?"

I could hear panic in Rick's voice. My mind was saying that probably nothing was wrong, but my gut was firing off alarm signals. I offered to call 911. But he was worried that she'd be furious if she was simply not answering her phone. I knew she lived quite close to me—I saw her out in the yard all the time. Although my response was highly unusual, it was governed by my proximity to her.

A minute or two later, I arrived at her elegantly landscaped home. I walked to the front door and rang the bell. No answer.

I walked around to the back and knocked on the door. No response. Her car was parked outside of the garage. I peeked in, just to be sure she wasn't inside.

Rick had given me the security code. Feeling like a burglar, I entered the numbers. The garage door groaned open to reveal a neatly arranged space and another door to the interior.

The house—tall ceilings, big windows—was absolutely quiet. No music or TV. Everything was very neat. Very tidy. I wandered around, calling her name.

The kitchen was large, with gleaming appliances. Kids' photos neatly covered the fridge, each one carefully labeled. The living area, just off the kitchen, seemed ready for company. The pillows were fluffed, and comfortable-looking knitted throws were artfully hung over the sides of a sectional sofa.

I kept calling her name, softly at first—I didn't want to overly alarm her if she was sleeping somewhere. Then, I began to call out more loudly.

I walked through a back hall to what I hoped might be the master bedroom.

She was in bed, lying very still, with an empty fifth of vodka and a half-full bottle of prescribed, potentially lethal benzodiazepines by her side. I dialed 911.

She could talk to me but barely. Her words came out in whispers.

"Natalie, I'm calling 911," I said.

"No... no," she muttered. "No hospital. Please don't call anyone. I'm fine."

She was far from fine. I called Rick while trying to keep her awake and talking to me.

Within minutes, the medics arrived. She didn't fight them. She was too out of it. After they whisked her away, I stayed for a while, trying to find my composure. I was rattled.

Everything in the house was in its place. The trash was empty. Pots and dishes were drying on the counter, the kitchen towel still damp. Children's toys were stacked in orderly bins by the sofa. Her bedroom, except for her bed, was impeccable. No clothes or shoes lying around. No paperwork piled on a desk in the corner.

It would've been a perfectly neat suicide.

That's the day I began questioning the traditional criteria for depression and, without necessarily realizing it, formulating the concept of *perfectly hidden depression*, or PHD.

Natalie was highly successful in her job, well known and well liked. She was an extremely hard worker at everything she put her mind to and a caring and involved mother. She volunteered at her kids' school and in the community.

She'd never talked about considering suicide. She had merely felt bogged down by how much housework there was to do, especially with Rick traveling more. She'd seemed more anxious and uptight than depressed.

In her early sessions, I'd learned Natalie had been sexually abused by her grandfather, but she'd never told anyone in her family; she only told me because I directly asked. She was dominated by her parents, especially her mother, whom she could never please. She'd been a tough gymnastics competitor as a child, winning all kinds of medals and awards. Her mother had come to every meet; her father was too buried by work to attend. After the meets, her mom would tell her what else she could've accomplished or what mistakes she needed to work on.

Natalie had chosen her current profession as an accountant because her dad was one. It had been "the thing to do." She worked in his office, obsessive about the quality of her work, while always available for clients' questions and concerns. She was growing to hate her job but felt extremely trapped by finances and responsibility.

She admitted anger, especially with her mom, but couldn't express it. Natalie smiled at the thought of relaxing or of not trying to be everything to everyone. She laughed, "When am I supposed to have time to do that?"

Her suicide attempt was a potent wake-up call.

Natalie was hospitalized and went into rehab. When she came back, we began to confront what her survival strategies had done to her.

The solution—to hide so much of her true self—had become the problem.

Natalie felt tremendous guilt about the suicide attempt. She had to accept that she'd been secretly hopeless. She worked with Rick on his own feelings about the attempt, and she finally began confiding in him about her real struggles. She needed time and space to work through the issues of her childhood, including the sexual abuse and her inner critical voice that constantly shamed her.

Natalie also worked hard on her sobriety. She set more defined boundaries in her relationship with her mother. She made plans to leave her job, which required huge changes in her mind-set, in her relationship, and in her finances. She knew she had to get out on her own and do something she loved.

Natalie's worth would no longer be about accomplishing tasks or achieving what others expected of her; her worth would develop out of learning who she wanted to be and what she cared about. She learned how to let go of her perfectionism, accept that she could get angry or tired, and recognize how intense shame had been governing her—all her life.

A year or so later, she felt ready to "graduate."

She was glad to be alive. Her smiles were real, her joy infectious.

Natalie's story has become a familiar one, as I've talked with many people just like her. If you've picked up this book, it may be very familiar to you as well.

I hope you'll join me in learning from her healing and the healing of others who've worked hard to get off the perfectionistic treadmill they've created or that was created for them.

It may save your life.

# Introduction

If you see yourself in Natalie's story, if you focus on counting your blessings and cannot admit or express painful emotions, if you're plagued by perfectionism and worry, if no one knows who you really are, then read on.

One Saturday morning in April 2014, I was thinking about patients like Natalie—and how their path to healing is very different than someone with a more classic presentation of depression—as I was writing my weekly blog post. In it I described someone who appeared to others to have a perfect life, but underneath that facade painful secrets existed. I noted how what can appear to be a blessed life can have its downside, and I briefly described what needed to happen therapeutically to loosen expectations of perfection. I called the post "The Perfectly Hidden Depressed Person—Are You One?"

I'd been blogging for a little more than a year at that point and would receive fiftyish shares on a really good day. By the end of that Saturday, however, more than fifteen hundred people had shared the post. I was told I'd gone viral. Much more important than that fact was that I'd apparently touched an emotional nerve, and the hundreds of emails I received following the post's appearance in HuffPost brought that revelation into even sharper focus.

I couldn't get that fact out of my mind. Just how many people were experiencing this kind of dynamic? I spent the next four years reading others' work on perfectionism and depression, and talking with expert researchers in the field. I interviewed more than fifty individuals who came forward after reading my posts on perfectly hidden depression and who volunteered to describe the pain of their own lives so that others could benefit. People started coming into my practice wanting help.

This book is built on all of those experiences, as well as more than twenty-five years as a psychologist. We'll be talking about the syndrome of *perfectly hidden depression*—a term that was created by me—what causes it, how it differs from classic depression, and what you can do about it.

As a therapist, I believe I'm a conduit between people: I share wisdom learned from those who've been hurt and found healing with those who are still lost and hurting. I want to pass on to you what I've seen in and learned from people just like you, people like Natalie, people who were silent for many years—until something made them come forward. I'll share their stories. The wonderful news? They got better. And you can get better too.

Two of the things you may fear most are exposure and loss of control, as you begin to consider dismantling the carefully executed life that you've created. We'll gently confront that fear. We'll balance a perceived loss of control with a new definition of *safety*—the safety found in self-acceptance, honesty, and openness. This book is designed to encourage you to make changes within yourself, whether or not you seek a therapist's help.

As you acknowledge your own ability and habit of covering up who you are, and as you begin to taste the freedom and fulfillment in honoring your entire being, powerful change is inevitable. What will unfold is your own complete emotional and mental potential, perhaps for the first time in your life. You can choose how and when to make these changes known to others whom you trust. But I will be encouraging you to begin looking for at least one person with whom you can begin to share your journey. As you step out of the prison of the perfect persona, you can discover the peace of self-acceptance and the strength within vulnerability.

I'm not trying to make this sound easy. It's not. Taking these steps will require courage. It may be hard at first to trust that these changes are even helpful. What could be wrong with being thoughtful of others? What's the big deal about working hard and expecting the best from yourself? There's nothing wrong with those things. However, when there's not a balance between giving to others and receiving from them—when shame invades your sense of worth, when vulnerabilities are seen as flaws—that's when perfectly hidden depression, or PHD, has entered the picture.

## Who This Book Is Written For

I'm sad to say that there is no age range, no gender, no race or religion that is immune to perfectionism and PHD. If the term "perfectly hidden depression" intrigues you; if you felt immediate relief, connection, or curiosity when you saw the title of this book; if your perfectionism is becoming far too burdensome, then this book is for you.

If you're struggling with suicidal thoughts, or if those thoughts emerge while you're doing this work, you need to seek immediate professional treatment.

If you're younger, you need to let an adult know that you're in big emotional trouble. Hopefully, *Perfectly Hidden Depression* will help you give yourself permission to do just that. But it's not enough support in such dangerous circumstances.

If you're a parent, read this book to guide your awareness and decision-making with your kids. Grieving parents of highly successful-looking teenagers have contacted me, tragically left to wonder, after that child took their own life, what they'd missed or what they could've done. Learning how to express the entire range of your own emotions will be an incredible gift to give to your children, for they will do as you do far more than they'll do what you say.

If you've watched with concern as your partner puts intense pressure on themselves on a daily basis, or you know of early trauma they've never discussed, reading this book may help you understand them more fully. You'll gain language with which to approach them about your observations and even influence them to read it for themselves.

If you're a therapist, this book will expand your thinking and challenge your assumptions about depression and what it can look like.

We—as individuals, partners, parents, doctors, and therapists—need to know the warning signs. We need to have a system in place to interpret someone's actions and beliefs, and not take what is superficially evident as the entire story. That system includes the recognition of perfectly hidden depression. Perhaps if we add PHD's lens to our camera, we can recognize when something's wrong and all be a part of healing.

## How This Book Will Help Guide and Support Your Healing

*Perfectly Hidden Depression* is written to educate, guide, and support you in your change and healing process. In Part I, we'll focus on understanding perfectly hidden depression. Chapter 1 will offer a definition of perfectly hidden depression and its key trait, perfectionism, while also identifying the ten primary characteristics of PHD. Even if you don't think of yourself as a perfectionist, you may find yourself in these other behaviors and beliefs. We'll uncover how perfectly hidden depression differs from healthy coping and classic depression in Chapter 2. You'll find a questionnaire in Chapter 3 that will help you assess where you belong on the spectrum of PHD and that can act as a helpful evaluation tool. We'll also discuss the stigma against revealing or seeking help for psychological problems, and how to overcome that fear.

In Part II, we'll switch gears and begin to work through the five stages of healing: consciousness, commitment, confrontation, connection, and change.

These healing stages offer a path for you to follow. But there's no "right" way to heal. Healing isn't one neatly designed task leading to another. The energy flow between the stages is circular, but it also travels inward, mimicking the spokes of a wheel. That's the way healing change happens. One aha moment may lead to a revelation in another stage. One mental block or seeming paralysis may lead to a breakthrough of emotion. All these guiding stages are uniquely important in creating more emotional and practical freedom, with an overall goal of increased self-acceptance and compassion.

What's most important in this, and in any other change process, is that you go at your own pace. If the work you'll be doing while

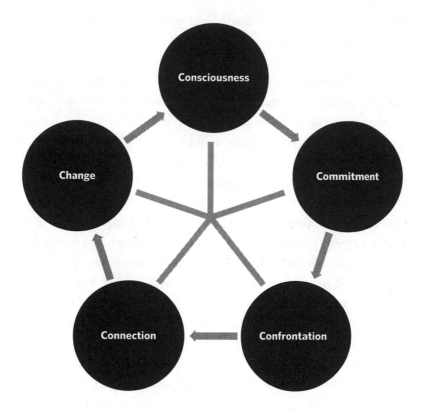

navigating the five stages becomes too jarring or painful, take a break. Realize that you're trying to alter a pattern that has protected and shielded you for years. It takes bravery and time to look at things differently and risk new behaviors. Please honor yourself. This is not something else you have to do perfectly. There's no perfect solution or perfect fix.

The last two chapters (Part III) will help you learn how to main-tain these new changes and help prevent backsliding into old painful patterns, both as an individual and within your relationships. The energy to create change and the energy to maintain change can be very different. We'll focus on situations that could potentially kick you into a perfectionistic spiral, and we'll discuss how to hang on to new learning at a time of increased stress. Predicting how these changes will impact your intimate relationships is a major factor here. Knowing how to approach and discuss this dynamic with your partner, your spouse, your family, and your friends can aid in these changes being welcomed and nurtured.

Interspersed within each chapter are exercises for you to do called *reflections*. Both introspective and action-oriented, these experiences are designed to move you forward. They may spark memories, emotions, or realizations that may be difficult to handle. Yet with each change you make, and every reflection that sheds insight, you'll create hope. And that hope will help quiet your fear and give you permission to continue risking and healing.

I can't highlight enough that the writing and recording of your experiences are a tremendous part of your healing. Therefore, my strong suggestion is that you maintain a separate journal in which to do the recommended writing. In it, you can regularly capture what changes you're noticing in your daily thinking or behavior, and record how you're being impacted emotionally, mentally, spiritually, or even physically. It's very helpful to keep all of that together not only for use in the present but also as a future reminder of how, perhaps very dramatically, your beliefs and behaviors have changed over time. Whether your journal is a beautifully embroidered book, a three-ring binder, or a folder on your iPad, it doesn't matter. If you're concerned about someone finding and reading it (as many people are), you can keep it at work, locked away somewhere safe, or you can use a journaling app with its own password. Please be resourceful.

Finally, the personal stories used in this book are taken either from interviewees who self-identified with perfectly hidden depression or from my own patients who've sought treatment. Their identities have been protected but their words are real. When asked why they wanted me to use their story, many stated, "I want to do everything I can to bring PHD to light, so someone else doesn't have to feel the way I've felt all my life." They want you to know you're not alone. They've also experienced your pain, and it's real. Please join them on this journey during which you no longer have to remain silent, and you no longer have to hide.

# PART I

# Understanding Perfectly Hidden Depression

CHAPTER 1

# What Is Perfectly Hidden Depression?

*You can't get to courage without walking through vulnerability, period.*

—Brené Brown, author of *The Gifts of Imperfection*

One day as Brittany—a tall, attractive young woman—came into my office, I wondered (as I always do in a first session) what problem or issue would come forth.

"I saw you on Periscope talking about perfectly hidden depression," Brittany said. "I've never been to therapy. But I know that you're describing me, and I've got to get help, because things are getting worse."

She stopped abruptly, seeming to immediately regret telling me even that much about herself. Smiling brightly, she sat a little sheepishly on the sofa, one of her legs nervously pumping up and down. She didn't know what to do, and she waited for me to respond.

"Well, if you identify with PHD, you're not used to openly talking about yourself. So I bet being here is hard."

She nodded, looking down at her feet.

I reassured her, "We can take all this very slowly. I'm here to listen, but you're in charge of just how fast or slow this goes. So, is there something that's happened recently that's made you more worried about yourself?"

Brittany didn't tell me everything about her life in that session. In fact, it was months before I knew her whole story. Occasionally, she'd blurt out a hurtful secret that she'd been keeping, all the while very closely watching to see my reaction, as she gradually took more and more risks in sharing her real life. Still, her ability to openly express the emotions connected to those secrets was very limited. I'd see only an occasional tear, quickly covered by a blank look or a change of subject.

And that's perfectly hidden depression. Shame, trauma, hurt, anger—so many of these experiences and feelings have been kept under wraps that opening up can be a slow process.

Brittany wasn't the first person I'd seen with this kind of emotional disconnect between the pain of what she was saying and the feelings she would allow herself to express. Others before her had shown this same kind of denial or detachment:

> Elizabeth recounted a story about waking to find herself lying naked on a beach, having been drugged and raped. "I've never thought the story was all that important. It was a long time ago," she told me, smiling hesitantly.

> Linda hadn't cried in years, even after her mother's sudden death. "Crying makes me uncomfortable," she said. "I think it's a sign of weakness."

> Jackson talked about strange, secret impulses to drive off the road, then followed his confession with, "I have a good wife and family. I'm just a little stressed."

Like the others, Brittany didn't look depressed in the classic sense. She was extremely rational and highly organized (if a bit rigidly), her planner stuffed with sticky notes and extensive to-do lists. She stayed very busy with dinners with girlfriends and a steady boyfriend. She was professionally successful, although highly anxious about making the right decisions for her future. She didn't look sad; in fact, she was often quite jolly and funny. What Brittany allowed others to see looked pretty perfect.

If you experience perfectly hidden depression, you don't recognize what's going on as depression. Depressed people are sad. Depressed people have no energy. Other people notice that they're listless or agitated, or that they sleep all the time. The very idea of you being depressed may seem ludicrous to you—at least before you started reading about PHD.

If you're completely honest, you can confess nervousness about what others would think if you admitted feeling down or hopeless. You fear the stigma against mental illness. You've said to yourself, *Oh my gosh, I'm not depressed. Crazy busy maybe. But not depressed.* You've handled pressure after pressure, loss after loss, and you've carried on. You've worked hard, parented hard, volunteered hard. You're always upbeat.

Most important, admitting depression would be admitting a flaw. And if you're perfectionistic, flaws are to be hidden.

You're like Brittany. And Elizabeth and Linda and Jackson. Because yours is not the classic presentation of depression.

No one suspects anything is wrong. Yet you're the person who might kill yourself, and no one would know why. Brittany told me months after our initial session that she'd been planning to take her own life before she walked in my door. She knew she couldn't live like she was living anymore, hiding so much pain and hurt, feeling hopeless and trapped underneath all that smiling.

It's depression all right. Perfectly hidden depression.

## The Ten Characteristics of Perfectly Hidden Depression

PHD isn't a diagnosis you'd receive from a doctor or a therapist. It's not a mental disorder. It's a *syndrome*, or a set of characteristics that, when they appear together, suggest a specific disorder or problem. You may have been aware, on some level, that something was going wrong. You might've searched online about depression, looking for answers, but you didn't find yourself in the criteria. You may have begun to question if the knot in the pit of your stomach was even real.

Psychologically, it's interesting to see how these characteristics—these behaviors and the beliefs underneath them—can serve a purpose. With perfectly hidden depression, that purpose is to shield, to protect, to survive.

Let's look at the characteristics of perfectly hidden depression. If you experience PHD, you likely...

- Are highly perfectionistic and have a constant, critical, and shaming inner voice

- Demonstrate a heightened or excessive sense of responsibility

- Detach from painful emotions by staying in your head and actively shutting them off

- Worry and need to control yourself and your environment

- Intensely focus on tasks, using accomplishment to feel valuable

- Focus on the well-being of others but don't allow them into your inner world

- Discount personal hurt or sorrow and struggle with self-compassion

- May have an accompanying mental health issue, such as an eating disorder, anxiety disorder, obsessive-compulsive disorder, or addiction

- Believe strongly in counting your blessings as the foundation of well-being

- May enjoy success within a professional structure but struggle with emotional intimacy in relationships

Does this sound like you? If you recognize most or all of these characteristics in yourself, you probably feel relieved to have a name for what's been your secret truth. That pit in your stomach is real. You're not just crazy busy.

But that relief may be followed immediately by additional stress as you consider the idea that your PHD could end up on your never-ending list of things to "fix." Please stop right there. Because while you'll gain the skills to deal with PHD, you'll also need to address your tendency to want to do this work perfectly.

Before going forward, let's stop and address this tendency.

### Reflection 1: Creating a Mantra of Confronting Shame and Perfectionism

As a reminder, the work you're asked to do in this book is *not* something you need to do perfectly. Be gentle with yourself. Allow yourself time, patience, and permission to make mistakes. The process of learning how to be far less self-critical is a huge part of the change you're creating.

Start out this reflection by opening your journal and taking a few deep breaths in a quiet, calm place. Ask yourself, *What do I need to remind myself of every day about my healing work with perfectly hidden depression?*

Play with creating a *mantra*—a mental reminder of a positive goal or experience you want to have. Your mantra could be, "Whatever time it takes is time well spent," or, "I'm going to relish discovering what I write."

Start a list of mantras or positive affirmations as you discover them along the way. If you struggle with this exercise, that's okay. Your mantra could be, "It will take time to be more positive with myself, and I'll keep my mind open."

Now, with your mantra in mind, let's go over in more detail each of the ten perfectly hidden depression characteristics. Keep in mind that some of these behaviors and beliefs in moderation are healthy. Taken over the top, they can lead to PHD.

### You Are Highly Perfectionistic and Have a Constant, Critical, and Shaming Inner Voice

You expect the best of yourself at all times. You spend hours making something error-free, slave over handwritten thank-you notes for every small favor done, and work until late in the evening, long after the kids have gone to bed.

In Rick Carson's book *Taming Your Gremlin: A Surprisingly Simple Method for Getting Out of Your Own Way* (2003), he offers wonderful illustrations of nasty little imaginary gnomes who viciously whisper shame-ridden things into the ears of their human victims, such as, "What makes you think you're any good? Anybody could do this job." Our gremlins are our critical voices, and if you're a perfectionist, they're a constant presence in your thinking. You may try hard not to listen. Yet they're evaluating your every move, incessantly finding fault.

Brené Brown's research on shame and her own experience with it led her to write about what she'd learned. Her best-selling works speak for themselves, reflecting just how many of us are vying for perfection—and losing that battle every day. In *The Gifts of Imperfection*, she defines perfectionism as "…a self-destructive and addictive belief system that fuels this primary thought: If I look perfect, live perfectly, and do everything perfectly, I can avoid or minimize the painful feelings of shame, judgment and blame" (2010, 57). She goes on to point out that perfection is impossible, as we have no control over how others view us. And the more perfectionistic we are, the more frantic we can become to achieve that impossibility. This sets up a painful cycle of immense effort, followed closely by intense self-criticism.

How can you tell if you're perfectionistic or simply striving for excellence? Let's say you're training for your first marathon. Do you tell yourself, *I'm training for the marathon, so I will bow out as finance committee chair for now*? Or do you say, *I'm training for a marathon. So I'll have to get up really early on Sunday morning to get that financial report done before the meeting on Monday*?

The first response reflects flexibility—you've added something to your plate and taken something else off, so you're not overloaded—and striving for excellence within realistic boundary setting. Hopefully you can hear the inflexibility of the second statement and how it's based on perfectionism and shame. Your gremlin is whispering, "You can't give up a responsibility. That would be selfish."

The frenetic pace at which many American families live today can certainly add to the likelihood of developing perfectly hidden depression. If your three children play two sports each, are in at least one club, and have homework, that's a lot of perfect snacks to prepare, essays to help write, and games to attend (not counting your own work). Yet you're likely to equate limiting your involvement or delegating responsibility with not being a good parent—you might even consider yourself a failure. As a result, your energy and effort level ramps up with each new task, and your exhaustion becomes one more thing to perfectly hide.

As you grow in your own courage to challenge shame, you'll work on how to let go, bit by bit, of the expectation of perfection. You'll find a way to quiet that shaming voice and listen to it only when it speaks for your conscience or in your best interest, not when the message is undermining and harsh. You'll trace how perfectionism became part of your very being and replace it with thoughts and feelings of acceptance of vulnerability.

### Reflection 2: Identifying My Shame and Giving It a Name

Find a quiet place to sit with your journal and take a few deep breaths. You might even close your eyes for a moment and focus on your body from head to toe, noticing where there might be tension or discomfort.

Allow yourself to think about the family and culture in which you grew up. Take a few moments to consider what you learned was shameful. What were you never supposed to do or feel? What was never allowed or supported?

Write down these inflexible, critical whispers. For example, you might hear, "It's selfish for you to put your needs first." If you can only think of one or two, that's fine. You'll discover more along the way.

You might even like to give that gremlin's voice a name, such as "Shirley" or "Bob." It can add a little humor when you hear "Bob's" voice in your head. As you go about your day, see if you notice the whispers.

## You Demonstrate a Heightened or Excessive Sense of Responsibility

If someone's going to take responsibility, it's you. You feel compelled to do it. You don't know how to say no. Your hand is up in the air to volunteer, to take charge. It's what you do. You fix things. You make things work. It's true that this habit may help you avoid an anxiety that springs from not playing a fixed role, like committee chair or host. But more likely than not, you can't remember a time when you didn't take charge.

Let's look at how Adam's extreme sense of responsibility developed. Note that if you suffered from parental abuse, his story may be emotionally triggering for you. Please read with care.

### *Adam's Story:* Becoming Über-Responsible

*Adam's most painful memory of his abusive dad was when he lined up all his children in order to find out who'd committed some misdeed. He held out a burning piece of paper so close to them that they could see and smell the scorch. Then he flicked on a cigarette lighter and forced them to hold their fingers to the flame, making them take turns until all the children were screaming with pain. Adam learned that if he admitted to doing the misdeed, he could stop his dad.*

*"It was a pivotal point in my understanding," Adam realized. "I could stop bad things from happening. I could fix it."*

*Adam became a rescuer of others and never, under any circumstances, showed his own anger. "It became part of the facade that I never got mad," he confessed.*

*Things seemed okay until he went to college, choosing his father's major. Although he was an honors student, painful feelings surfaced, and Adam became secretly suicidal. He quit college, feeling as if he'd failed horribly.*

*Ever the rescuer, Adam married his first wife after having met her only once—she needed a way out of a desperate situation. When he remarried, he chose someone quite mean and spent much of his life dedicated to protecting his children from the explosive destructiveness of their mom.*

*It was years before he could see his depression as "an illness, not a weakness." Adam gradually made the vital connections between his past and his present, and could begin to recognize his own intrinsic worth.*

On this journey, you'll also slowly find your own value, not only in what you do but in who you are.

### You Detach from Painful Emotions by Staying in Your Head and Actively Shutting Them Off

Being vulnerable scares you. You believe that if you start crying, you'll never stop. So you'll jump through hoops to detach from any intense emotion and remain more analytical.

Patricia wrote to me: "I don't feel sad, but I don't feel happy either. And if you asked, I don't think I could remember the last time I felt actual joy." Like Patricia, you primarily stay rational and objective, muting both ends of the emotional spectrum.

This doesn't mean you never get angry. In fact, when it comes to having control over things, you can get pretty worked up. But overall, you're not comfortable with conflict, so you'll withdraw or avoid it if at all possible.

This detachment requires *compartmentalization*—the mental act of storing emotions or thoughts away from your present awareness. You've shoved away so much pain that you may not recognize it when it's trying to emerge.

Let's say you had to care for your siblings due to your mom's alcoholism. You really didn't have a childhood. Now, in rearing your own children, confusing emotions tug at you, as you provide them with the care that you never received. But you don't recognize that tug for what it is—pain from your own childhood.

You may even deny emotional pain of any kind. You might tell yourself, *Things just don't bother me.* You've stuffed all your painful experiences and memories into boxes and shoved them far away in some remote closet in your mind. The boxes gather dust and are rarely, if ever, opened. Jane proudly revealed to me: "If [my pain is] too big for the box I have, I make a bigger box."

Perfectionism researchers Gordon Flett, Paul Hewitt, and Samuel Mikail point out that, "When asked what they are feeling, [perfectionists] will typically *describe* their feelings rather than *express* their emotions" (2017, 236). In other words, perfectionists *talk about* being afraid or disappointed. Feeling it, *being present with the actual emotion*, is another matter. That's why when you choose to talk about something hurtful or painful, you do it without much emotion. You describe, you don't express.

You admit, "These layoffs are pretty scary." But you detach from the actual fear. "Joe's mom's death was so unexpected. It's been hard," you hear yourself say. You loved your mother-in-law, but not a tear is shed, at least not publicly.

Eventually, something can rip that box open. And what comes out is unsettling and highly potent. You won't share it or you don't know how. And that can lead you to intense loneliness and despair— even the consideration of suicide.

*Stefan and Sadie's Stories:* When the Box Rips Open

*Stefan believed that he had everything under control. His career was booming. His kids were doing well, all high achievers. He felt his marriage was solid, even though the couple hadn't gone anywhere without the kids in years. He reasoned, "That's simply what has to be for now." Everything was going to plan. It took immense effort to pull it all off, putting him under constant pressure. But it was worth it. Or so he believed.*

*But then, Stefan suddenly felt as if he couldn't go on. More quickly than he could have possibly imagined, he found his thoughts traveling at breakneck speed, going from a need to live life full throttle to not wanting to live. At all. He explained, "I sat in the garden with a gun in my mouth determined to do it. I have no idea why I didn't. I just didn't. Outwardly, I have it all.*

*But I'm dead inside and feel often as if I'm just going through the
motions. The only thing that stopped me was my kids."*

Stefan had been taught that a real man never lets anyone
see him sweat. And he'd followed that rule—almost for too long.

Sadie had a similar dive into suicidal darkness five years
ago, just before her thirty-ninth birthday. And for similar
reasons as Stefan. No one would hear her complain. No one
would know her struggles.

She recounted, *"I was seconds away from driving my car
into the path of a tractor trailer. What stopped me was seeing
the driver's face. I realized he would think he killed me, and my
pain would simply be transferred to him. I couldn't be responsible
for that. The next day I went to my doctor and, for the first time
ever, spoke freely about what I learned later was anxiety and
depression. I'd been seeing my doctor for over fifteen years. I
remember the pain in her eyes as she said, 'I had no idea. Why
didn't you say anything?'"*

This next reflection will start you on the path of recognizing
which emotions have seemed too difficult or frightening for you to
feel or express.

### Reflection 3: A List of Emotions

Grab your journal and take a few moments for this brief list-writing exercise. You'll refer to this list later, so be sure not to skip it.

Breathe some calm breaths and then write down the emotions, in
order, that you find most difficult to feel. Afterward, take a moment to look
at your list and see what feelings, if any, emerge. Write them down.

### You Worry and Need to Control Yourself and Your Environment

Rationally, you can only feel responsible for what you have
control over. But you can't trust that others will be as careful as you

are; you worry it won't be done well. So you take control to avoid that worry. The trap that you fall into? You'll take charge of the care of an elderly parent—so you won't worry. You'll plan the volunteer charity walkathon—so you won't worry. You'll volunteer to do school pickup every day—so you won't worry.

A cycle is established. Worry leads to a need for control, which leads to taking more responsibility, which leads to exhaustion, which leads to hidden anger or resentment.

And what's your defense against anger or resentment?

More control.

Some worriers actually believe that their worry is keeping their world safe, as if it's the same thing as thinking ahead or trying to prevent problems before they occur. Those mental exercises help. But worry is your brain on a treadmill going over and over the same things, actively aiding in the avoidance of emotion.

Do you worry all the time? Give some attention to the next exercise.

**Reflection 4: "I believe that worry…"**

Once again in your calm place, and with your journal, please write out the words, "I believe that worry _____." Fill in the blank. Be honest. Whether the statements seem rational or irrational, write down what function you believe worry serves. For example, "I believe that worrying is part of being responsible. My dad always worried." Or, "I believe that if I worry about the future, I will be able to better protect my kids." See how many statements you can make about worry. Great job!

These reflections will all come together to build a picture of where you've been and where you're going.

## You Intensely Focus on Tasks, Using Accomplishment to Feel Valuable

Accomplishment is the major way you earn a sense of pride or esteem. You think, *I can't leave things unfinished until tomorrow. It drives me crazy!* This belief, coupled with your innate perfectionism, means you have a really hard time relaxing. You doubt that you're valuable simply because you exist. You believe that you have to bring hors d'oeuvres to a party to be welcome or lead the food drive to be respected. Your *wants* and your *musts* are confused. You don't stop to ask the question, *Am I doing this because I want to, or am I doing it because I'm afraid not to?* You can experience tremendous insecurity if you don't feel as if you're accomplishing enough.

That same insecurity is likely to cause you to shrug off compliments or accolades. Even if everyone calls the accomplishment "perfect," you're going to punch holes in whatever you've done. A compliment may rest briefly in your heart and in your head. But since it's not absorbed by a matching inner sense of secure esteem, it fades away. It's never enough.

### Reflection 5: Saying Thank You

As you begin your day today, try this assignment: If anyone says anything complimentary to you today, all you're going to say is "thank you" and not another word. Watch carefully and see what happens.

When you get home, and you're in a calm space with your journal, write about what it felt like to accept a compliment without side-stepping or discounting it. This may be harder than it sounds, but it's an important step. Keep up the great work!

### You Focus on the Well-Being of Others but Don't Allow Them into Your Inner World

Staying focused on others is something that you feel bound by duty to do, and yet, your caring is sincere. Simultaneously, that focus serves as a safety shield that diverts attention away from you.

In fact, you'll flatly avoid letting others see into your heart and mind. You keep almost everyone's access to you very superficial. Friends might or might not recognize this—or you may have attracted friends who are great receivers (they respond mostly when you focus on them) but not very good givers (they don't reciprocate the attention you give them). You keep others very distant from knowing anything too intimate about you. It helps you avoid pain. After all, if you received a deep, warm hug, or someone noticed the shadows under your eyes, it might ruffle the veil that guards your perfect facade.

If you pretend that you have no immediate needs, that your role in life is to give and rarely to receive, then the loneliness of not being noticed or loved well can be ignored. At least for a while.

### Reflection 6: My Circle of Friends and Family—Does Anyone Really Know Me?

Go to your calm space with your journal. For this reflection, you're going to draw a set of nested circles, the first one fairly small, the second a little larger, the third largest of all. The smallest one will end in the center. Now draw dots on those circles representing significant people in your life.

Your inner circle, people who are closest to you, are found in the smallest circle. Write their names by the dots that represent them. Be brutally honest. The next circle represents a lesser sense of connection, and the outer even less. Yet be sure that you list individuals who have some importance to you. You'll be referring back to this reflection, so be as thorough as possible.

After doing this exercise, journal about how it felt to distinguish who's in your inner circle and who isn't. You might also write about any circles you'd like to create that don't exist at the moment.

### You Discount Personal Hurt or Sorrow and Struggle with Self-Compassion

You've been discounting for years whatever hurt or pain happened to you, whether in the past or in the present. You reason, "There are people a lot worse off than me." Why? Because at some point you learned: *If I focus on myself or my needs, I'm being self-centered. If I ask for something I want, I'm being selfish.*

So what distinguishes self-centeredness from selfishness? Someone who's *self-centered* finds a way to make everything about them. They might say, "Oh, I'm so sorry that your mom has cancer.

That's horrible. Will you still be able to take on that account?" Or, "Wow, congratulations! I'm so happy you're pregnant! It took me four years and so much money for infertility treatment. I wouldn't know what doing it naturally feels like." Does this sound like you? I doubt it seriously.

*Selfishness* is putting your own needs before someone else's most or all of the time. Someone who's selfish rarely thinks of anyone but themselves. They have little to no empathy. What a selfish person desires governs their thoughts and actions. Does this sound like you? You may have told yourself yes. But rationally? Not at all.

Two skills you'll need to combat feelings of self-centeredness and selfishness are self-awareness and self-compassion. *Self-awareness* is simply keeping in mind your own needs or wants and considering them important. They may not be your top consideration all the time, but they're on your list. And you treat them respectfully. Being self-aware is good self-care.

*Self-compassion* is about acknowledging whatever pain or trauma you experienced and recognizing its impact on your life—without drowning in blame or bitterness. Self-compassion doesn't equate with feeling sorry for yourself. Nothing could be farther from the truth. On your way to healing, using this book as your guide, you'll be learning about how self-compassion works—recognizing that anyone going through what you did, learning what you learned, experiencing what you experienced would've been hurt or damaged in some way. That's not becoming a victim. That's not wallowing in blame. That's acknowledgment of your experience.

Men especially have been taught that it's unmanly to show tenderness for the self. Both genders learn the same in their families: "Don't cry over spilt milk." "You made your bed, you lie in it." "No one likes a whiner."

Whining isn't what we're talking about.

## Riley's Story: Finding Self-Compassion

*When Riley was seven, her adored mother died from breast cancer. Riley's father, who'd been fairly active in her life, threw away all the pictures of her mom and wouldn't allow Riley to speak of her. There was no violence, no alcohol abuse. But her father's grief turned bitter, and he would take it out on Riley. He'd chide, "You'll be lucky to get a job at Walmart the way you're going." He'd scoff at her free throw attempts in basketball: "I thought they were free." He mostly stayed away from her, providing for only her basic needs.*

*Riley grew a very thick skin and would allow no one access to her inner self. She came to despise vulnerability. In spite of this, people were drawn to her. She was tall, smart, and quite witty. Riley married a guy who was extremely calm, and she went to medical school and became an oncologist. She also had children, although she lost one to a very late miscarriage. Her response? "I got up the next morning and saw patients."*

*She began taking her anger out on her husband and was often critical of his mistakes or irritated that he seemed okay with her always taking the lead. The irony of the repetition of her father's behavior didn't escape her, but she found it hard to control.*

*Before reading about perfectly hidden depression, Riley said, "I knew I didn't have Major Depression. What I mostly felt was a numbing loneliness. The more I did things well, the more pressure I felt not to fail." But after reading about PHD, she said, "I am there. I am that person."*

*Riley had never grieved, not only for the death of her mother but for the emotional loss of her father at the same time—a pain she'd masked for years. Her father was eventually diagnosed with depression, and she slowly developed compassion for what both of them had gone through. One night, she shared all this with her husband, and they began to turn their relationship around.*

Riley learned that recognizing hurt from the past wasn't whining. It wasn't about blame. Self-compassion involves acknowledgment—taking the time to realize the truth of what really happened and how it would affect anyone. You were vulnerable then, and you have vulnerabilities now due to what happened. You can learn to accept and begin to work with those very vulnerabilities.

### You May Have an Accompanying Mental Health Issue, Such as an Eating Disorder, Anxiety Disorder, Obsessive-Compulsive Disorder, or Addiction

Struggles with shame or fears surrounding control can affect people in many ways, especially if there's trauma in their past. For some, it can grow into actual psychological dysfunction. Eating disorders, along with panic, anxiety, and obsessive-compulsive disorders—even addictions—can all be linked to this struggle. For this reason, we find these issues co-occurring with perfectly hidden depression fairly often.

We'll talk much more about these co-occurring disorders in Chapter 4. What's important to realize on this beginning leg of your journey is whether these disorders are present in your life. You're good at minimizing your struggles, so you want to avoid making the mistake of labeling yourself with "perfectly hidden depression" when there may be a psychiatric problem present that shares features with PHD. Your journey ahead could be made more complicated if serious untreated issues exist. You may need to take additional time to address them while traveling forward. Overall, however, the healing work in this book can be helpful to all, as it addresses basic acknowledgment and acceptance—two very healthy gifts for anyone to give themselves.

Let's hear how difficult it was for Jacki to give up what had been helping her to hide for years.

*Jacki's Story:* Complete Denial

*Jacki grew up believing that her beloved mom hung the moon. So when her mom said that Jacki should never wear more than a size 2 dress, that became her mantra. When she was sexually fondled by an uncle, her mother said, "Well, he didn't mean to do it. I'm sure he's sorry." The day after she hid in her room, avoiding her stepfather's rage, a cute dress magically appeared, as if to reward her for her invisibility and her silence. When Jacki cried after not making the cheerleading squad, she was told that tears didn't belong in the family.*

*As a result, Jacki never cried. Jacki rarely ate. And Jacki went through life silent, extremely thin, and perfectly hidden. Jacki learned that staying in control was her identity. "You can never be too thin," she reminded me, smiling.*

*She married the right guy. She volunteered in the community, earned a great reputation in her corporate job, and made the lives of her children active and productive. Gradually, she began seeking treatment for anxiety—she worried a great deal—and was given sedatives.*

*Jacki denied anorexia but admitted her hair was beginning to fall out. "It's harder to make a Brazilian blowout look decent," she laughed. And she was using more and more medication to help calm herself down. She'd read about perfectly hidden depression, had been curious, and was drawn to the idea that someone could be hiding so perfectly that no one could see.*

*"I used to hide in my room and pretend I was invisible," Jacki confided. "But you're saying that no one has to stay invisible."*

*Yet, when she began admitting the anger that lay beneath her very chiseled surface, she left therapy. Jacki was gone— choosing to remain hidden.*

Jacki was in active denial about her anorexia, her abuse, and her intense need to stay in control. It can take tremendous courage to confront your denial. You're on that path now. Give yourself credit for beginning a process that will, at times, be emotionally strenuous. It may take all your effort not to go back and hide under a familiar rock.

## You Believe Strongly in Counting Your Blessings as the Foundation of Well-Being

Good things that occur in our lives are true blessings. It's healthy to be grateful. It's what I call "swimming around in the glass half full." It's positive. Optimistic.

Yet the habit of gratitude, overutilized, may deny you the chance to recognize the underbelly of a blessing. What do I mean by "underbelly"? I mean something that may not be apparent on the outside but is present just the same. Think of a rock that you see on a path. You never see the bottom side of the rock, yet it exists. It's just as real as the part you do see.

Here's another example. Let's say you're quite wealthy. You may have a lot of insecurity about others being mainly attracted to your bank account. The insecurity is the underbelly of the wealth.

All blessings have an underbelly. Yet you can feel disdain for yourself for admitting it. Add in the tendency to call your problems inconsequential or silly, and you can get stuck in rigid positivity. Next, add moments of not always feeling positive—such as having fantasies about getting in your car and driving away from this pressure cooker that is your perfect life—and you can easily build a concoction of heavy guilt and shame. How could you ever consider leaving? Just how ungrateful are you?

What this journey will bring is a change in those beliefs. Every good thing has inherent loss within it. You can be ecstatic about your cancer remission *and* need to grieve what chemo did to you. You can be delighted that your four children are doing well in school *and* admit that keeping up with homework eats up a lot of time. You can be glad you found a new job *and* miss some of the perks of your old one.

You can learn how to grieve *and* be grateful all at the same time. A glass is half full and half empty by definition. It's important for you to learn how to connect and disconnect with the feelings from both.

If you're a spiritual person, you may struggle with feeling as if you're suffering because your faith is weak. You can become, in your own eyes, a failure as a believer. If this is your situation, I highly recommend that you seek spiritual counsel.

### Reflection 7: The Underbelly of Blessings

In your calm space, write out the blessings in your life. You can pick tangible things, intangible things—anything that is a blessing. Please be as specific as you can be. Write out *how* it's a blessing to you. For example, "Jane is a blessing because she's so funny and makes me laugh."

After you've written down as many blessings as you want, go back and ask yourself, *What's the underbelly of this blessing?* To continue the previous example, it might be, "Sometimes I don't know if I can share something more serious with Jane." This isn't throwing Jane under the bus. What it means is that every blessing has an underbelly. For every gain there's a loss.

Finally, write about what this reflection has pulled up for you emotionally. What beliefs did it challenge? How uncomfortable were you in doing it? This is harder to do than it seems, especially when perfectly hidden depression is entrenched. If it doesn't come easily, that's okay. Challenging beliefs that have been around a long time can be very difficult. You're doing the work, and that's what's important.

### You May Enjoy Success Within a Professional Structure but Struggle with Emotional Intimacy in Relationships

You appreciate structure. Whether it's within the organization of a corporation or the hierarchy of the PTA, you've been very successful. You're known as a leader. You push yourself to do well. You thrive on projects that need control, order, and predictability.

Healthy intimate relationships generally require flexibility, openness, and spontaneity. True connection requires vulnerability. You need to control what others know about you—and that gets in the way of emotional intimacy.

Hiding can become quite complicated. Lauren told me, "I have two very different groups of friends. With one, I'm the party girl. I drink, cuss, and cut up, because they all do. Then I have another group. We meet for coffee or maybe one glass of wine. We talk about work and girl things. No one in either group knows each other. No one knows there's another side of me." For Lauren, there is no real intimacy going on. She is silencing half of herself to be with each group, fearing rejection. Because she can't accept herself as who she is, she is living a life in which no one really knows her. And she is horribly lonely, although surrounded by "friends."

Annie's story drives home this point.

### *Annie's Story:* Learning the Value of Vulnerability

*Annie had a binge-eating disorder for years, triggered initially by being cruelly criticized about her growing teenage body by a ballet instructor. She began making herself vomit then. She was in therapy for this and making good progress.*

*Annie had seriously dated a guy named Carlos and then suddenly broke up with him. "I don't know why," she said. "He was perfect in so many ways. But I was bored." Their relationship had been extremely superficial, as she hadn't told him anything real about her. She'd only revealed who she needed him to believe she was. Annie had hidden. Her gut knew there was a problem but not truly what it was. So she'd ended the relationship.*

*After our work on her perfectly hidden depression, she saw Carlos at a reunion and approached him. She wanted to give herself and their relationship another chance. He risked coming into her life again, though he'd been very hurt by the breakup. Suddenly, it wasn't boring at all. She told him about her struggle with food, self-esteem, and many other things that she'd kept to herself. At last contact, they were talking about getting engaged.*

*And Annie was no longer bingeing.*

**Reflection 8:** My Reaction to "Perfectly Hidden Depression"

Congratulations! You're through the first chapter! Today's exercise is an open writing reflection, and the topic is simple: What was your reaction when you read the term "perfectly hidden depression" for the first time?

Maybe the first time you encountered it was when you bought this book. I'd like for you to explore the term's impact on you. Did it make you sad? Did you find relief? Did you become frightened of exposure—of someone finding out? Please write freely as you chronicle your journey.

Maybe this story will make you smile. On a Colorado highway many years ago, on a family trip during which I'm sure I was stuffed in the backseat between my two brothers, I remember seeing signs for a diner called "Pete's." Every five miles or so, there would be a reminder that Pete's was right around the corner. Several miles down the road came the last sign: "Now you've done it. You've just passed Pete's." I remember my dad chuckling.

So now you've done it. You've read through the first chapter. There's no going back. You didn't listen to whatever voice might have whispered, "No. Keep going the way you are. Don't think about changing. You're fine." You've begun the trek to discover what's hidden underneath your smile, how to express those feelings and challenge those beliefs. The next chapter will focus on the differences between healthy coping, depression, and perfectly hidden depression, and hopefully add to your understanding of PHD.

# CHAPTER 2

# Healthy Coping, Depression, and Perfectly Hidden Depression

*Thus this "tower of strength," this "rock of Gibraltar" took his own life on Tuesday, July 20, 1993…*

—Sydney Blatt, on the suicide of Vince Foster

How many times have you heard yourself say, "I'm fine, thanks," when you knew that you weren't fine at all? I'd bet a lot. When I began writing about perfectly hidden depression, many people emailed me with their reactions to giving PHD a definition. Their responses reflected relief, gratitude, even shock. One expressed, "I can't believe how you're describing me. It's like you're in my head."

I'm certainly not the first person to describe that depression doesn't always appear the same from person to person. Sydney Blatt, quoted above, was one of the first to gather research on perfectionism and its link with depression and suicide. He suggested that certain types of depression should be identified through someone's lived experience rather than whether their symptoms fit official criteria. The term "perfectly hidden depression" reflects this same thought: the official criteria for depression don't have to be exactly met for depression to exist.

Not all of the emails or comments I've received have been supportive. In fact, some have been fairly critical: "Isn't it bad enough that people are having to deal with real depression? Now you're lowering the bar?" And: "I think you're trying to talk a lot of people into thinking there's something wrong with making the best out of life's suffering. I call that courage and strength—not a psychological condition." And then there's this: "It sounds like you're describing someone who's empathic as well as a good decision maker and leader—and you're saying that's not a healthy way of living life. I resent that."

The last thing I want to do is discount the pain of depression, pathologize inner fortitude and strength, or find fault with being a caring, giving person. Yet my attention to perfectly hidden depression has been greatly spurred by the rise of suicides in the United States and internationally. Jean Twenge, a notable researcher and sociologist, has studied the behaviors of every generational group from the WWII generation to baby boomers to the iGens (her term). She notes that depression and suicide are dramatically rising in teens. "As teens have spent less time with one another in person, they have also become less likely to kill each other. In contrast, teen suicide rates began to tick up after 2008… 46% more teens killed themselves in 2015 than in 2007" (2017, 87).

The National Center for Health Statistics has sounded similar alarms. The overall rate of suicide is the highest it's been since 1986, rising 24 percent from 1999 to 2014, showing highly dramatic increases in women and men ages forty-five to sixty-four. But every generation's numbers, except the most elderly, rose substantially (Curtin, Warner, and Hedegaard 2016).

In order to try to stem this tide, all potential presentations of depression must be considered. And because perfectly hidden depression can mask itself as "healthy coping," let's discuss the differences between actual healthy coping, depression, and PHD.

## The Skills of Healthy Coping

Whether we're born with certain gifts or skills or we learn them along the way, we each gather skills or strengths—things we do competently—and carry them around in our psychological toolbox to use when we need them. As an example, perhaps organization comes easily to you; you methodically design your approach and follow through when meeting a deadline. Or perhaps you're someone who waits until that deadline is looming before you get something done; you're most effective in a time crunch. Neither is particularly "better" than the other one. Both can be considered skills.

We handle stress through the use of those skills. It becomes the way we function. For example, when a sudden death occurs in the family, some immediately focus on what needs to be done. Others are far more comfortable expressing their grief in the moment. Still others deny any pain at all or even seem angry; this latter group may not have a constructive skill to handle grief. What's in our psychological toolbox helps us deal with life—both the good and the not so good. Our tools, or skills, develop over time and with practice. And sometimes there are tools missing.

*Healthy coping* is using constructive skills to deal with whatever comes our way, from the joyous things in life to the more painful. Anger management is a skill; self-soothing or calming yourself down is a skill; processing information rationally is a skill.

When facing loss, disappointment, fear, anger, grief, shock—if you're someone with healthy coping skills, you'll get through it. You may not think you can. You may want to be anywhere but where you are. You may have big questions and complicated feelings, but you see your way to the other side. Whether it's through spiritual faith, your support system, or working diligently on emotional survival, you get through.

Healthy coping involves the compartmentalization of feelings. As mentioned in Chapter 1, compartmentalization happens when you store feelings in your emotion closet for the moment, as you tend to the more pressing things that need your attention. But when it's safe, when you have the energy, when you have privacy, or simply when you have time, you connect with those feelings, good or bad. You recognize how they're affecting you. And if they're painful, you risk sitting with hurt or sadness, darkness or despair, in order to heal. That is coping with strong emotions in a healthy way.

How do we all learn to compartmentalize? Healthy parents soothe their children, and those children learn that feeling sad or bad is tolerable. We watch those same parents soothe themselves. We learn through their modeling (as well as from other adults) that emotions don't have to govern our lives, that there's a time and a place to express them. Healthy parents teach their kids about feeling pain and working through it a bit at a time.

You may have heard some version of the Sukuma proverb, "The wind does not break a tree that bends." Connecting with your strong thoughts, experiences, and emotions that you had to store away for a time is, in essence, bending. You recognize on a very basic level that you can't survive the storm if you're overly rigid.

If your coping skills are healthy, you can bend. You can express vulnerability. You can feel all emotions. Your tree won't break.

But if you struggle with perfectly hidden depression, your logic is backward. No one modeled heathly compartmentalization for you. Instead, you believe that you'll break if you bend—if you admit vulnerability or hurt. Let's begin to challenge that thought. This next reflection will suggest what might be waiting for you in your emotion closet. We're taking this very slowly. But again, I remind you, please go at your own pace. If you're not ready to do this reflection, come back to it.

### Reflection 9: Taking Stock of What's in My Emotion Closet

Take some time to breathe deeply and settle into your calm place. Sometimes it helps to close your eyes and create an actual calm scene in your mind's eye. What do you see, what do you smell? Then allow yourself a few seconds to drink in the calm.

Now imagine yourself standing in front of a closet that is filled with memories or experiences that you've never delved into emotionally. Just notice what's on the shelves and hangers and inside boxes. Write out what you recognize is there. Realize this might be emotional for you. Take it slow and steady. If it's too hard, don't worry. If you don't recognize anything, that's okay. We're going to come back to this reflection in a much later chapter. Remember, this takes practice.

You might also want to give that experience a number from 1 to 10 and predict how difficult that experience might be to connect with emotionally. For example, if you were raped in college and that memory has been hidden in your closet completely untouched, it might be a 9 or a 10. Other painful experiences might not be as dramatic but still be important. For example, if you have a learning disability and school was very hard for you, or you had a stepparent who never paid attention to you, these long-standing experiences may rank very high.

You can certainly have healthy coping skills and still experience perfectly hidden depression. PHD is on a spectrum and, even if present, it doesn't mean that you don't have wonderful healthy qualities innate within you.

### Reflection 10: Acknowledging My Strengths

Please take a moment to sit and identify the strengths you already possess. Acknowledge those that will help you learn and practice the new ideas and behaviors in this book. Which have helped you in the past and are positives in your skill set? Patience? Consistency? Humor? Curiosity?

You might go back to your mantra from your very first reflection and remind yourself of what's going to give you hope and encouragement along the way. You're doing a wonderful job!

## What Perfectly Hidden Depression Is Not

Before we go any further, it's important to clarify three potential misconceptions about perfectly hidden depression so that you can more confidently go forward and uncover what's underneath that perfect persona you show others. Hopefully, these three ideas will help create a better definition of what perfectly hidden depression *isn't* and what you *shouldn't* expect of yourself through this process.

### PHD Isn't a Recognized Diagnosis or Mental Disorder

Let me stress again: perfectly hidden depression isn't a diagnosis. It's not a mental disorder. It's a term I've created to describe a syndrome (a set of behaviors) that can mask true depression. It's not a term found in any psychiatric or psychological textbooks. Yet many people have asked, "Where can I go to get help for perfectly hidden depression? If I tell my doctor I have PHD, will they treat me for it?" The answer is likely no—not because practitioners don't understand the complexities of depression but because those experiencing PHD may not offer the familiar or expected answers that those with a more classic depression might give. They may pick up on your perfectionisim, but unless you fully explain, "I'm not what I seem to be," then your depression could easily be missed.

Here's a near-tragic example.

*Sam's Story:* Not Asking the Right Questions

*Sam decided to see a doctor to get help because, in his words, "I was getting too close to the edge. The doctor was a pretty cold, aloof kind of guy. He gave me a depression inventory instead of talking with me, and I answered, of course, like someone with PHD. The inventory asked if I felt hopeless. I wasn't about to admit that, so I checked no. For someone like me, the question should be, 'If you felt hopeless, would you tell anyone?' The answer would still be no. But we could've talked about PHD. He was assuming I'd completely open up to him.'*

*"I attempted suicide the next week. Surprisingly, that same doctor visited me in the hospital. 'You masked your feelings,' he said, his tone inferring that I should blame myself for not being truthful. My answer was, 'You didn't ask the right questions.'"*

Nothing is gained by blaming the mental health profession for being governed by its criteria. If you don't tell a doctor or therapist exactly what's wrong, how can they know?

By traditional standards, to be diagnosed with clinical depression at least one of these two major criteria (plus a handful of others) have to be met:

1.  A noticeably depressed mood for most or all of the day, for several days in a row, or

2.  What's termed *anhedonia*, the lack of pleasure in previously pleasurable activities. (We'll describe this in more detail in the next section.)

If you don't meet these criteria, it's more than likely you'll fall through the diagnostic cracks. You've heard the old saying, "If it looks like a duck, swims like a duck, and quacks like a duck, then it's probably a duck." If you head over to your local doctor or therapist, they're not likely to diagnose you as a duck. You don't look, swim, or quack like a depressed person. You don't fit the criteria. Instead, you'll be told, "You need to slow down." "You don't seem depressed." "You're pretty anxious. Take this pill to help you sleep."

Some clinicians will get it. They're thinking outside the box, picking up on your ever-present smile, sensing the huge pressure that you carry on a daily basis, watching and waiting for more-normal emotional expression that rarely emerges from someone with perfectly hidden depression. They notice. And they ask the right questions.

### PHD Isn't Always Easy to See in Yourself

As children, we're born into a country, a region, a culture, and a family. These factors shape our parents' view of life and thus our own. Children are loved on a spectrum of very well to very poorly. If we're lucky, both parents are mature, giving, and stable people. But you may not have been so lucky.

Whatever their situation, all children do what they can to survive emotionally. That may sound dramatic to you. It may not be actual physical survival that's at stake (although in the most horrific families or environments this could be true). It's emotional survival. Given what was yours to face, you came up with a strategy for coping. Siblings, reared in the same home, can adapt differently. One may rebel. One may try to please or make people laugh. One may work to fix the situation, and another may become invisible.

You didn't recognize your own strategy as a strategy. It simply became you. People may have said about you, "Oh, that's just Jason. He stays out of the way." Or, "You can always count on Gail." Underneath the obvious, superficial behavior was an unconscious strategy, and it's likely to greatly affect you now in the way you approach your life.

So, perfectly hidden depression may not be easy to see in yourself. For many, it's not. Even if someone, such as your partner, points out how you didn't cry when your friend died, or how you seem more and more uptight about how the kids are doing in school, or how you're constantly busy—none of that sinks in. You say, again, "I'm fine. Really. It's all good."

Many people who identify with perfectly hidden depression tell me that they searched online about depression. Their gut was telling them something was wrong, they just didn't know what. But they were puzzled at what they found. They said, "I didn't see myself in what I read. I'm really active, I think pretty clearly, I enjoy my kids." So they dismissed the idea of depression and pummeled themselves with more shame for wondering. Again, the problem lies in having to fit clinical criteria.

Fiona's story reminds us that it's harder than you think to recognize perfectly hidden depression in yourself—until it's almost too late.

*Fiona's Story:* If I'm a Star I'll Be Loved

*Fiona demonstrated her great sense of humor from the first minute of our interview. She joked, "Do you know what a holler is? I grew up in a holler in West Virginia."*

*Fiona was the daughter of an alcoholic dad and a drug-addicted mom. Her home life was filled with chaos, her mother using Fiona to pass drug tests. The only person who cared for Fiona was her maternal grandfather. Yet, she thrived at school, explaining, "It was the only way anyone would see me." Fiona also mothered her little sister, who even now says, "You were always there." Later her mom got sober, but the damage had been done.*

*In high school, Fiona was an outstanding softball player, yet no one acknowledged that feat in her family. She got a full scholarship to college and married at eighteen. When she left, the futility of her efforts at being loved caught up with her. Not eating, not sleeping well, she googled "symptoms of depression" many times but wasn't able to find herself in required symptoms such as anhedonia. She was busy. Highly involved. Driven.*

*After her first therapist looked at her and said, "You don't have depression," Fiona felt so alone that she broke. She became suicidal, her husband coming home to find a knife in her hand.*

*Fiona has now found another therapist and is working toward health. She stated, "Self-compassion at times feels pointless. I'm not accomplishing anything. I've had a one-way relationship with so many people. When I tell someone how I feel, it's uncomfortable."*

Like Fiona, you're beginning to unwrap what have been long-term strategies and long-held beliefs. You're allowing feelings to surface that have been long suppressed. And like Fiona, it's not going to be easy. Give yourself credit for doing the work.

### Reflection 11: What Were My Survival Strategies?

Find your calm spot and breathe a bit. Start to think back on your childhood. In your journal, think of yourself as having played a role in your family, like you'd play a role in a play. If this is hard for you, think about your favorite TV shows or books and ask yourself, *What roles do the different people play? What function do they serve within the different relationships?* Then go back to your childhood. Were you the funny guy or the fixer? Did you get labeled the smart one or the one who did anything to stay out of trouble? What was your role? What function did it serve for you or others? Did it keep you out of trouble? Did it distract you from the chaos of your surroundings?

Write about your childhood role. Then ask yourself, *Am I still playing that role? What might happen if I changed roles or stopped entirely?* This role became your survival strategy. Feel free to add other ideas as you gain more perspective on your past. If you struggle, ask a family member what they remember about you.

## PHD Isn't All of Who You Are

You may have many healthy coping skills in your skill set. But if you identify with perfectly hidden depression, some of what you consider a skill or solution may actually have morphed into a problem. Yet you don't want to make the mistake of throwing out the baby with the bathwater, as the saying goes. Counting your blessings and being grateful is positive. Working hard toward a goal or striving to do your best is far from pathological. Thinking ahead, predicting what concerns or dangers there could be—a close cousin of worry—has a definite place in problem solving.

As I've stressed before, the characteristics of perfectly hidden depression, in moderation, can be helpful. But when they begin to govern every aspect of your being, they can become a huge problem. It becomes self-destructive when your perfectionistic critical voice is screaming at you nonstop in the background. When obsessive worry takes over and pressures you into working feverishly for control, that worry is no longer constructive in any way. Somewhere in you, there's a gut understanding of what's happening. Whatever has been positive and helpful about the behaviors and beliefs you've used for years to cope has now crossed the line to unhealthy. And you can begin secretly feeling a loneliness and lack of true connection that's intolerable.

**Reflection 12:** Which of the Ten Characteristics of PHD Will Be the Hardest to Change?

In order to begin to let go of something, you have to understand its worth to you. Does giving it up or changing it involve too much loss? Or is it balanced by the gain made? In this reflection, refer back to the ten characteristics of PHD listed in Chapter 1. Then rate them from 1 to 10, with 10 being the hardest to consider changing or the one you've relied on the most. Then list them in order in your journal.

If you feel ready, you can write about how they've protected you as well and what you fear might happen if you alter them in any substantial way. You can also consider which characteristics you've taken over the top and which you've kept in moderation.

Additional work: If you're feeling up to the task, refer to Reflection 11, What Were My Survival Strategies? Reread about the role you played and may still be playing. How are these two reflections connected? Please take some time to consider and journal your thoughts.

## Perfectly Hidden Depression Versus Classic Depression

Trying to explain the core of clinical, or "classic," depression, Andrew Solomon, author of *The Noonday Demon: An Atlas of Depression* states, "The opposite of depression is not happiness but vitality…" (2001, 443). You can develop a complete or near-complete lack of engagement with the basics of living. Brushing your teeth can seem like a mountainous task in severe depression.

**Clinical depression** is characterized by a melancholy mood lasting for several days. It's on a spectrum, ranging from moderate to severe. *Moderate depression* means that symptoms must be present in adults for two years, and for one year in children. *Severe depression* means that symptoms need only be present for two weeks but cause major impairment.

According to the DSM-5 (American Psychiatric Association 2013), clinical depression must include at least *one* of these primary criteria:

- A noticeably depressed mood for most or all of the day
- *Anhedonia*, or the lack of interest in previously pleasurable activities

Plus four of these additional criteria:

- Foggy thinking or indecisiveness
- A general slowing down of mental and physical activity
- Problems with goal setting
- Sleep and appetite disturbance
- Feelings of hopelessness or helplessness
- Expressions of low self-esteem and worthlessness
- Fatigue, agitation or irritation
- Thoughts of self-harm

When you're clinically depressed, you don't feel like "you" anymore. Those who love you are aware that something is wrong or off, that you're not your usual self. They're concerned. They'll ask, "Are you okay? What's wrong?"

When I watch a patient emerge from clinical depression, it can feel as if I'm getting to know a new person, not the one who initially walked through my door. Their eyes twinkle a bit, they're laughing at their own jokes. They notice things in the room that they've never noticed, because they're not consumed with their own internal chaos. It's like coming out of a dark cave and becoming accustomed to the light.

When you experience perfectly hidden depression, your loved ones may have a hard time seeing your struggles and pain. Living with PHD can be a very lonely journey. Since you're such an expert at hiding, it's not likely that someone is going to say, "Hey, are you okay? You don't seem yourself." Unless you want them to. Unless you're finally ready to talk about who you really are.

It's only when someone with PHD begins to identify their pain and commit to healing that their depression might be revealed. When you're doing the very difficult work of learning how to express very raw and painful emotions, or when you're allowing someone else into your actual world, you change.

When I see someone emerge from perfectly hidden depression, it can also feel as if I'm getting to know someone new, but in a very different way than with clinical depression. I hear about feelings long suppressed that are now being expressed. I see tears of relief. I hear about anger that's finally being respected. The wondrous change I see emerges from increased freedom of expression and a deepening of self-compassion. This is now your journey.

You can glimpse how this important work can change your life in Tony's story.

### Tony's Story: Shame

*Tony was born into a wealthy Virginian family. He was the quarterback of his football team, homecoming king—basically, Mr. High School. His mother pushed him to play violin, which he hated. But like everything he touched, he had to excel, eventually giving a senior recital. He recalled, "She would tell all her friends that I was so good at everything—that I was a great son. I couldn't take that away from her."*

*In the final seconds of the game for the conference title, he threw what he thought was a well-timed pass. His receiver couldn't get to it. The only thing said by his dad afterward? "Let's go home." No comfort was offered.*

*Tony lived his adult life completely defined by what he perceived others expected from him. He began to secretly seethe about always having done the "right" thing. Sadly, he acted out his anger instead of recognizing the prison he'd created for himself. He began having affairs.*

*After Tony's wife found out, he became actively suicidal and was hospitalized. Then he began outpatient work, and the perfectionistic prison in which he lived his life became obvious. In therapy, his sessions couldn't go a minute overtime before he stood up abruptly. At one point, an alternative treatment for anxiety and trauma was discussed. He refused, saying he didn't know if he would do it correctly.*

*Tony was highly involved with his kids and well liked for his apparent easygoing style. But he was filled with shame about mistakes he'd made with no way to express that shame. One day he confessed, "I saw a picture of myself the other day when I was about four. I felt an overwhelming desire for that child to stay a child, where he could always think of himself as successful. I wanted to say to him, 'You're going to make such big mistakes, buddy. Just stay four.'"*

*Tony began letting go of his intense inner critic. He made connections with what he'd been trying to avoid feeling. He learned that his own being was important. He slowly learned words for feelings and that they were important to voice. And he actually stopped watching the clock, allowing the session to end more naturally.*

## The Difference Between Healing Classic Depression and Healing PHD

With classic depression, a primary goal in the healing process is to reconnect the person with their external world—to reengage with their family, their friends, and their purpose; to stop the withdrawal and the implosion of their very being; and to ease the misery of hating themselves and their life.

Let's stress that many of those with classic depression have fought just as hard as those with perfectly hidden depression to "hide" their problems, maintaining their lives and shouldering their responsibilities. They've gone on with their jobs and taken care of their children, while fighting to put one foot in front of the other every day. They've struggled to find the right medication, keep their job afloat, search for a helpful therapist, or find time to exercise. It's been a constant, difficult battle. Many who suffer the symptoms of classic depression have kept quiet about how hard that battle has been.

With perfectly hidden depression, the overall goal of healing is to connect the person with their internal world—the world of their rigid beliefs and hidden emotions. First, you have to identify the ten characteristics of PHD as problems, and second, you have to commit to change. That may sound easy, but it's not. The fear of change can be overwhelming, and over and over again you'll have to revisit your commitment.

If classic depression is a lack of vitality, perfectly hidden depression is a lack of self-acceptance. Self-acceptance is the antidote for PHD as you learn and practice compassion for all the various aspects of who you are, from your recognized strengths and capabilities to your insecurities and vulnerabilities, and from your pride and accomplishments to your sense of remorse and regret.

So what is holding you back? A main reason is your need for others to believe that nothing makes you falter, nothing causes you to stumble, that you're an impenetrable rock of a person. Remember how Tony feared doing a new therapeutic technique imperfectly? The tears that sprang up in his eyes showed the depth of his despair at being seen as out of control or flawed in some way. You may have similar feelings. But part of the healing process is to allow yourself to experience your flaws and accept them.

Let's see what happens if you try on the concept of self-acceptance in this next reflection.

### Reflection 13: What Does Self-Acceptance Mean to Me? Identifying My Fear

The practice of self-acceptance is core to healing from perfectly hidden depression. It's time to reflect once more with your journal in hand.

When you hear the word "self-acceptance," what does it mean to you? What are you telling yourself that implies?

Write "If I accept myself, then _____." Fill in the blank with what you predict might happen, both welcome and unwelcome things. A welcome consequence might be: *If I accept myself, then I won't feel so pressured all the time.* But there could also be an accompanying fear: *If I accept myself, then what happens if I don't push myself and I disappoint?* Please journal or make a list about what you believe the gains of self-acceptance could be, as well as its feared losses.

You should be very proud of yourself that you've read this far, as you're combatting that fear at some level. Good for you. I know it's scary.

### Can You Be Classically Depressed and Have PHD Simultaneously?

Can perfectly hidden depression and classic depression coexist? Remember, perfectionism can be part of many mental illnesses. Its presence doesn't point necessarily to perfectly hidden depression. But if you've been living the life of PHD, your own fatigue level, loneliness, and despair can deteriorate, over time or with enough stress, into clinical depression. You can run completely out of steam. That may occur through some external trigger, such as losing your job, or some force causing you to feel terribly exposed and as if you've failed. Or it can be caused by an internal trigger—maybe your child has reached the age you were when your own sexual abuse began, or your own self-destructive thoughts have begun to seep into your everyday existence.

Your depression, successfully hidden until now, can become impossible to contain. Like Brittany and Tony, you too can realize that you've got to find another way of living. You're on that path now.

In the next chapter, you'll find a questionnaire to determine where you fall on the spectrum of perfectly hidden depression. And we'll talk about overcoming stigma and accepting your PHD.

# CHAPTER 3

# Overcoming Stigma and Recognizing Perfectly Hidden Depression in Yourself

*I knew if I admitted the truth, that I had just had a panic attack, it would expose me as a fraud, someone who had no business anchoring the news.*

—Dan Harris, author of *10% Happier*

Dan Harris, anchor on ABC's *Good Morning America*, was on live network TV when he had a major panic attack. In the quote above, you can hear his ensuing fear of the potential repercussions for the career he'd spent a decade building—because his vulnerability was exposed. He used that experience to help guide him to learn meditation and develop an entire new way of life, which he talks about eloquently and with great humor in his book, *10% Happier: How I Tamed the Voice in My Head, Reduced Stress Without Losing My Edge, and Found Self-Help That Actually Works—A True Story*. I highly recommend his book for anyone trying to discover their inner calm while fearing that that very goal will compromise their ability to thrive and achieve. Sound familiar to you? I'm sure it does.

His words mirror what I've heard from others. When I asked Joe why he'd never revealed his hidden depression, he replied, "I've lived a very calculated life. I don't want to be treated with kid gloves, with every shortcoming earning the question, 'Are you on your meds?'"

You can hear Joe's fear that he'd be closely scrutinized for any sign of "illness" or perceived as needing special treatment. Perhaps you also fear that you'll be defined by and rejected for any sign of psychiatric struggles. No one wants to be identified or classified as one aspect of themselves, be it their gender, their race, their religion, or whether they're tall or short, big or little. Your worry about rejection and discrimination may be so extreme that you don't seek treatment or else hide behind a pretense of everything being okay.

When you add perfectionism in with this fear of stigma, it could be years before you come into treatment or pick up a book like this one—if ever at all.

And you have lots of company.

### Reflection 14: What Are My Feelings About Mental Illness, Really?

Getting into what's hopefully now an easy and calming ritual for you, take a few minutes with your journal to write down how you view people with mental illness. From the mentally ill homeless man gesturing wildly, talking to himself as he walks down the street, to the neighbor who tried to kill herself, what do you say to yourself about the lives they may have lived?

When you hear that another celebrity is talking about their mental illness, what are your reactions? Do you admire them? If so, why? If not, why?

Are you comfortable with your thoughts? Or do you want to change them? If the latter, how do you want to change them?

## Struggling with Stigma

Jenny Lawson, otherwise known as The Bloggess, has been revealing her own mental illness and confronting the prejudice against it for years. In her book *Furiously Happy*, she eloquently remarks, "In the years since I first came out about struggling with mental illness I've been asked if I regret it…if the stigma is too much to handle. It's not… it's strangely freeing… In a way I'm lucky" (2015, 319).

Let's look at what you might be afraid would happen if you risked allowing more of your complete self to be known.

### Reflection 15: What Am I Most Scared of Revealing? And to Whom?

For this exercise, please refer to Reflection 6, My Circle of Friends and Family—Does Anyone Really Know Me? Beginning with each person from your outer circles and working your way in, ask yourself, *What am I scared that they will think or feel if I'm more open about myself and what I struggle with?*

This task will probably get harder the closer you get to your inner circle. That's quite normal. Because you have many more interconnections with those in your inner circle than the ones in your outer circle, taking risks in those relationships may cause more conflict or upheaval—or at least that's what you may fear.

Your worries may not be rational, however. In fact, the people in your inner circle may welcome your openness and the changes it brings. Breathe. Allow yourself to feel as you write. You're doing so well—this isn't easy work!

Since you're reading this book, you're likely someone who's been hiding for years. And confronting your fear of stigma is a huge part of the healing process.

### The Immense Risk in Revealing and Not Revealing PHD

In perfectly hidden depression, the fear of being found out is immense. In more than a third of the interviews I conducted, the interviewees were out in their backyards or garages, talking quietly on their phones so no one could hear, or they were behind locked doors in their offices.

Brittany, from Chapter 1, stated flatly early in her treatment, "You know, I can only tell you these things because I know you'll lose your license if you tell anyone else. So I'm safe."

Julie sadly admitted, "I would never have even said these words before I came to see you. They were in my mind, but *never* would I have allowed myself to utter them out loud."

That lonely silence can be a death sentence in the most severe cases. Let's talk briefly about the studies on the severe dangers of perfectionism. There are far too many to quote here, but it's important to point out that highly qualified researchers have been working on this issue for years.

Perfectionism as a psychological problem was first described in 1984 by noted educator and psychologist Asher Pacht. Then in 1995, Sydney Blatt (quoted in Chapter 2) continued the discussion of its risks. Edwin Shneidman, the founder of the American Association of Suicidology, in his book *Suicide as Psychache: A Clinical Approach to Self-Destructive Behavior* (1993), proposed that what he termed "psychache" (unbearable psychological pain) was associated with suicide more than simple depression. That concept led others to look at the relationship between perfectionism and psychache, and Ricardo Flamenbaum and Robert Holden (2007) found that there was a strong connection between socially prescribed perfectionism and suicidality.

So what is socially prescribed perfectionism? In their recent book, well-known researchers on perfectionism Flett, Hewitt, and Mikail (2017) divide perfectionism into three groups: self-oriented, other-oriented, and socially prescribed. *Self-oriented* is expecting yourself to be perfect; that striving comes from within you. *Other-oriented* is expecting others to be perfect. *Socially prescribed* is when you feel immense pressure from others to be perfect; it follows the logic that basically the better you do, the better you're expected to do. This last category is especially dangerous—not that the other categories can't be—because it can create a tremendous sense of hopelessness, the psychache that Shneidman discussed, and a major factor in suicidal behavior.

You can identify with all three forms of perfectionism, just two, or primarily one. If you live with any of them, your awareness of stigma and need to avoid recognition is likely more than troubling. Let's stop and give you a chance to journal about your own awareness of where your perfectionism lives within you.

### Reflection 16: What Category of Perfectionism Do I Find Myself In?

Let's consider for a moment the three categories of perfectionism: self-oriented, other-oriented, and socially prescribed. We're getting a little more in depth here, so take your time. Remember, there's no right or wrong.

Can you tell if your need to be perfect comes only from within you— that it's a striving for excellence on steroids? If so, when did it become important?

Are you perfectionistic with others? If you are, is there someone from whom you expect their best at all times? Are there others you "let off the hook"? What's the difference between them and what does that suggest to you? Do you expect from others what you expect from yourself? How does it feel to admit this to yourself?

Who in your world expects perfection from you? Or who in your past expected it?

What's it like to consider the differences between all three categories? Have you ever considered that your perfectionism could put you in danger?

Your fear of being found out can be so immense that even at a doctor's office or psychiatric hospital you may not tell. Benita almost lost her life due to that fear.

### Benita's Story: Hiding Almost Too Well

*As a child, Benita was gregarious and highly energetic. Her father, who took that as disrespect, would threaten her mother, "I'm going to break the contempt I see in her eyes." He began sexually abusing Benita on a regular basis, while she lived out a complicated, love-hate relationship with her mom, who knew about the abuse. By thirteen, she was wishing for her own death.*

*Benita became a promiscuous teenager (a common response to sexual abuse) before escaping through marriage to a violent man. She desperately covered up his abuse and tried for years to create a "white picket fence" life. Benita still would not be broken.*

*But one day she became hysterical in an ob-gyn's office; her sexual trauma was triggered by a pelvic ultrasound, and she was taken to the hospital. Benita was given meds to calm down, no one asked any questions, and she got back to her life. She said not a word to anyone. She was "fine."*

*Although Benita had three kids by age twenty-five, she divorced and went to college, receiving a full scholarship. She thrived, was immensely popular and respected, and was put on multiple task forces and committees.*

*"I was totally doing the PHD thing," Benita stated, "but things got increasingly worse. I could be hysterical at home, when I was alone, and no one could see. But I was totally in charge when I got on campus. I was walking a tightrope. If I overachieved, everyone would think that I was normal."*

*Years later, as Benita finally talked about the mood swings she experienced almost on a daily basis, she was diagnosed with a form of bipolar disorder. It was a diagnosis that took a while for her to accept. It had taken a serious suicide attempt before the doctors ever asked the right questions. "All those years, I was depressed but hid it. People thought I was so entertaining."*

It's so easy, when you're reading Benita's or anyone's story, to see what needed to happen for her to change direction or to get help. Her hysteria at home could've been a lot of things: a response to past trauma being triggered by parenting her own children, the pressures she was under as a single mom, or mood swings. Yet her need to look as if she had it all together almost overwhelmed her very life.

Perfectionism and being frightened of stigma can work together to create not only denial but a virtual seesaw of days when you look put together and in complete control, but then, with enough pressure, times when you explode in a burst of frustration.

### The Ever-So-Important Fight Against Stigma

Help may be arriving from an unexpected place: the younger generations.

Today, mental illness and the secrecy surrounding it is being uncloaked by everyone from Hollywood celebrities to British royalty. Millennials seem much more aware of the vital importance of maintaining mental health and are seeking therapy more openly. Mental health awareness Twitter hashtags abound and have attracted thousands of shares. Websites that feature not only "experts" talking about mental illness but also those who are living with it are gaining huge popularity. There's a monumental effort going toward modernizing attitudes and providing the public with unprejudiced mental health education. Celebrities and others who can make a difference are coming forward, choosing to reveal anxiety, severe depression, postpartum depression, eating disorders, or bipolar disorder. They're modeling for the world that you can be highly competent in your field and still manage mental illness.

Perfectionism specifically is being challenged on some of our major elite college campuses, in protest of the marked increase in student suicides. The students themselves are confronting the unspoken message that you're not supposed to struggle, appear lost or frustrated, or reveal that your studies are actually very difficult for you. After all, you're a student at Stanford or Penn. You're above all that. You were smart enough to get in. It should be no sweat.

How are they challenging this myth?

Stanford's online student academic coaching newsletter, *The Duck Stops Here*, describes their own version of perfectly hidden depression as the Stanford Duck Syndrome. Caroline Beaton (2017) quotes a pinned post: "Everyone on campus appears to be gliding effortlessly across this Lake College. But below the surface, our little duck feet are paddling furiously, working our feathered little tails off… Frustration, anxiety, self-doubt, effort, and failure don't have a place in the Stanford experience." For Stanford students, the duck syndrome represents a false ease and fronted genius. They've even formed a Duck Stop Advisory Board to build a structure where students can reveal themselves openly and honestly without fearing penalty or rejection.

Then there's the Penn Face. Julia Barr (2016) wrote in *The Tab*, the student-led online journal at Penn State, "The Penn Face is the pressure to always present yourself as if you have all of the pieces of your life in order. It's the pressure to say you're OK and act OK even when you don't feel OK. Everyone reacts to the Penn Face differently—some adapt to it naturally, some spend all of finals week in their rooms to avoid it, and for many, it takes a serious toll on their mental health, stability and ability to cope." Christine Vendel (2018), reporting on yet another suicide at Penn in 2018, continues with the shocking statistic that fourteen suicides occurred between 2013 and 2016, more than twice the national average. Students won't go to counseling centers because of the stigma and the culture of perfectionism.

Heath's story makes it all too evident that hiding suicidal thoughts can happen to anyone at any age. Fighting this tremendous prejudice and misinformation is paramount, both culturally and individually.

### Heath's Story: Tragedy That Could Have Been Stopped

*Heath grew up in a well-to-do family and attended a high school where many kids' goals were to go to an Ivy League school. And many parents pushed. Teachers focused heavily on standardized test scores. But Heath seemed above it all. He did extremely well academically. People loved being around him. He was close to his mom, who wasn't one of the pushers and who encouraged him to do anything with his life that he wanted. He looked as if he had it made.*

*The school counselor was contacted by one of Heath's friends, Angela, who'd gone to camp with Heath. She warned that Heath was suicidal, based on several texts during the last few weeks. The counselor called Heath in and asked him some questions about it. Heath, embarrassed and surprised at being called into the counselor's office, denied feeling that way and said Angela was exaggerating. It was just high school stuff. The counselor responded, "I see you every day laughing with your friends in the cafeteria. You look as if you're doing great. I was just checking." The counselor did nothing more.*

*Heath killed himself a month later. He didn't leave a note. His family still has no idea what his demons were. Perhaps he'd felt more pressure than they'd realized. Perhaps... perhaps... perhaps. Angela told them what she knew, which wasn't all that much. Heath's family would never be the same.*

### Reflection 17: Considering the Potential for Suicide

Please pause and write about what you just read. What do you take from Heath's story? Does it make you worry about your own children or what you may be modeling for them?

Do the facts about rising suicides frighten you? How do you feel about the fight against the stigma of mental illness? How in the context of a book on perfectly hidden depression are these questions even important?

Finding your motivation for change will be vital, because those very changes will be difficult. Your perfectly hidden depression has been there for you day after day, week after week. It's helped you survive. So, you'll need support. And that's when the fear of how others, even loved ones, might respond can be paralyzing.

Part of the healing process is moving beyond this fear. Savannah said, "If I let people know what I feel inside, if I let anyone know what's in my head, I will never be seen as competent by them again." That's the same thing Dan Harris initially feared. Yet they both decided to take that risk.

In this process, you will fail. You will falter. Not every day will lead to a success. You will relapse into old behaviors, catch yourself, and keep on going. To help you, you'll need to create a support network, even if it's one person—someone who you trust, will not judge you, and will support your journey. It won't be easy for you, but you will need to allow this someone to see you struggle.

In what may seem like a huge shift in topic, I'm going to tell a personal story. After three years of infertility treatment, I was blessed enough to get pregnant. One day at my ob-gyn's office, I was complaining about my swollen feet. He looked at me, lips pursed in disapproval, and said, "You worked hard to get pregnant. You shouldn't complain." Luckily, I didn't let his statement get to me. I returned his look, and said, "Yes. I worked hard to get pregnant, which means I have even more right to complain about my feet." He looked a little sheepish at that point and agreed with me.

You want to change your life. That's why you're reading this book. But it will be hard. Talking honestly about the underbellies of those blessings or how you barrage yourself with shame will feel strange and awkward. Talking and opening up in itself will feel vulnerable.

This may be a self-help book. But this isn't a journey you can take completely alone. You'll need a cheerleader who you'll allow to see the real you. It's time to begin wondering just who could be on your team.

### Reflection 18: Who Will Be on My Team?

Settling in once again into your calm space, jot down names of people with whom you might share that you're addressing your perfectly hidden depression. It may be someone in your inner circle, or it could very well be someone who's not so close, someone whose life isn't quite so intertwined with yours. You might be inclined to be more honest with someone who lives in another city—a longtime friend or someone from college. But it's ideal for that someone to be locally available to you. That said, if long-distance vulnerability is all you can do right now, then that will be great. You're taking small steps, and you want to go at your own pace.

Choose someone who will be capable of listening about how your perfectionism has been a prison you've been living in. And about how scary it is to break out of that prison. Try to visualize what it would be like to let that someone in on your real self. Write down what you might say. Allow yourself to feel whatever comes as you do so. Are there fears about what they'll do with the information or how it might change their thinking about you? Please try to decide if that's your own fear of talking or a rational thought.

## A Special Note to Teenagers

Considering opening up about your perfectly hidden depression may be even more frightening if you're a teenager or young adult and still dependent on your parents. If you're currently living in a situation where you feel the need to look perfect, you're likely to feel quite trapped. Parents may revel in your apparent success and happiness, or they count on you to be super responsible. They don't know what's underneath. How could you possibly tell them that so much of what they see is an illusion?

It's vital that you realize they're likely living on automatic pilot. All seems to be going to plan. They see no warning signs. They're respecting your privacy and not reading any journal that you might be keeping about your actual feelings. If you're giving them hints, they may still see you as only mildly struggling. It can be true that they painted a world for you that needed to look perfect. But your honesty with them might lead them to look at the mistakes they've made as parents—at their own imperfection. Nothing is worth your depression and sense of being trapped getting worse. Nothing.

You may also fear their reaction. And if they're neglectful or abusive in any way, you may have good reason for that fear. Sadly, parents are not always the people you can trust. However, you can find someone who will listen and help. Please don't make the mistake of believing that your darker feelings are normal or that they won't get the best of you. They can—and you may not have the opportunity to look back on how you feel now and say, "Wow, that was tough. But now I feel better." Talking with friends is fine. But opening up to someone who has the power to help can literally save your life.

Now it's time to assess where you fall on the spectrum of perfectly hidden depression. And we'll compare your earlier reflective journaling with what the PHD questionnaire might further reveal.

## Discovering Where You Fall Within the Spectrum of Perfectly Hidden Depression

Before you answer the questionnaire, please revisit Reflection 12. In your journal you identified the ten characteristics of PHD that you've most relied upon. You rated them from strongest to weakest in your own repertoire. Simply refresh your memory about these traits.

Each of the questions that follows is linked to one or more of the characteristics but reflects more of the actual behaviors or beliefs of perfectly hidden depression and perfectionism. If you have trouble with the "yes" or "no" aspect of it, you may be trying to answer too "perfectly." And if you think, *How I would answer would depend on the day*, then you're probably overthinking the process. Simply answer in the most accurate way you can.

Your score will give you an idea of where you fall on the syndrome's spectrum and the breadth of how many ways the syndrome has affected your choices. However, given how much we've talked about perfectly hidden depression, the questions themselves will probably not surprise you. Take your time, try to be honest, and remember: this isn't something you have to do perfectly.

### Perfectly Hidden Depression Questionnaire

1.  Do you struggle with confiding in others, especially about your real-life difficulties and problems?

    Yes _____    No _____

2.  Do you obsess about things looking perfect, both for yourself and through others' eyes?

    Yes _____    No _____

3.  Do you avoid talking to your partner or friends about feeling hurt by them or about a growing resentment you might have?

    Yes _____    No _____

4.  Do you have trouble sleeping or turning your mind off at night?

    Yes _____    No _____

5.  Do you have trouble admitting when you're feeling overwhelmed?

    Yes _____    No _____

6.  Do you push yourself to get the job done, regardless of the cost to you?

    Yes _____    No _____

7.  Do you spend most of your time analyzing or problem solving rather than expressing emotion?

    Yes _____    No _____

8.  Do you respond to the needs of your friends even when it can short-change your own?

    Yes _____    No _____

9.  Did you grow up in a family where feelings of sadness or pain were avoided, or where you were criticized or punished for expressing them?

    Yes _____    No _____

10. Have you ever been hurt emotionally, physically, or sexually and told no one? Or if you did tell someone, were you not believed or supported?

    Yes _____    No _____

11. Did you grow up in a family (or are you still experiencing a family) in which you felt as if you had to meet defined expectations rather than being allowed to be yourself?

   Yes _____     No _____

12. Do you like to have control of a situation if you're going to be involved?

   Yes _____     No _____

13. Do you have a growing sense that it's becoming harder to maintain an organized structure in your life?

   Yes _____     No _____

14. If so, do you feel anxiety or even panic?

   Yes _____     No _____

15. Do you tend to not cry or rarely cry?

   Yes _____     No _____

16. Are you considered ultra-responsible, the one who can always be counted on by your coworkers or family and friends?

   Yes _____     No _____

17. Do you believe that taking time for yourself is selfish?

   Yes _____     No _____

18. Do you dislike it when people consider themselves "victims," when they claim that it's not their fault when something goes wrong?

   Yes _____     No _____

19. Did you grow up being taught that you were supposed to handle painful things on your own? That asking for help reflected weakness?

   Yes _____     No _____

20. Do you strongly believe in focusing on the positives in your life or "counting your blessings"?

    Yes _____     No _____

21. Do you have a critical, nagging inner voice telling you that you're not good enough, or that you could have tried harder, even though you accomplished your goal?

    Yes _____     No _____

22. Do you outwardly seem hopeful and energetic while, at times, you struggle with a sense of being trapped?

    Yes _____     No _____

23. Do you make lists of tasks to get done during the day? And if they are not completed do you feel frustrated or like a failure?

    Yes _____     No _____

Count your positive answers to the questions above. If you answered yes to five to eight questions, you're likely a very responsible person, though you may need to consider taking more time for yourself. A yes response to nine to twelve questions indicates that your life is being governed by highly perfectionistic standards, which may be detrimental to your well-being. Thirteen or more positive responses may reflect the presence of perfectly hidden depression, or a depression that you deny. If your score is in the high teens or twenties, and you use this book for change, reading and working on your perfectly hidden depression may literally save your life.

## Reflection 19: What I Learned from the Questionnaire

What was it like to take the questionnaire? Given what you've read thus far, probably not much surprised you as far as the questions were concerned. Are you surprised by your score?

Look at your writing for Reflection 12. When you look at your answers to the questionnaire, do they alter how you may have rated the characteristics in Reflection 12? Are you relieved? More concerned? More convinced?

Hopefully, the questionnaire better defined how perfectly hidden depression can affect your daily decisions and behaviors.

Let's go forward with actual healing strategies, ideas, and guidance. We've stressed in this chapter that perfectionism isn't your only enemy. Another foe is the fear of stigma.

### Reflection 20: Why Am I Doing This Work?

In the introduction, I stated that hope would be your motivation to do the difficult work of opening up, admitting, and revealing all of who you are. With each insight, with each inner confrontation, with each emotional connection, you'll find greater and greater hope. Your hope will offer the courage to continue. Here I'd like you to write out the reasons that are motivating you. Is it loneliness? Is it fear that you'll pass this pattern on to your children? Is it a growing sense of desperation? Are you making connections from your past and seeing there might be another way to live your life?

Allow your mind and your heart to discover what will keep you to the task. Consider whether the following statement reflects your current truth: "I want my own life to be more fulfilling—to reflect who I really am. I'm tired of hiding." Write down your own version of this mantra and claim it as your own.

Good work. This is far from easy.

*Note:* If this work is stirring you up too much, or if you're having thoughts of hurting yourself, then this self-help book may not be enough. Please go to a local therapist or your family physician and talk with them honestly. The stakes are far too high. I realize that asking someone with perfectly hidden depression to do this seems contradictive. But this book—or any book—alone can't protect you from that kind of harmful thinking.

If your emotional state is stable and you've identified your support network, I invite you to move on to the next chapters—to learn even more about how to unmask your depression and work through it. Great work so far! I hope you congratulate yourself for already beginning. In fact, doing something nice for yourself as a thank-you is healthy self-compassion and self-care.

# PART II

# The Five Stages
# of Healing

## Consciousness, Commitment,
## Confrontation, Connection, Change

## About the Five Stages

*"Maybe, even at the end, she wanted to control her story... Even in her suicide, which seemed to convey the message that life had overwhelmed her, Maddy apparently still cared about projecting a collected, determined image."*

—Kate Fagan, author of *What Made Maddy Run*

Whatever has occurred to you as you've learned about perfectly hidden depression, I hope it includes a growing sense that you're reading this book with a purpose in mind. And that purpose involves healing. Healing from trying to look and act perfectly. Healing from hiding. And healing from depression. It's only after you begin to unwrap your own tight layers of perfectionistic packaging and discover what's inside that true understanding can emerge.

Think of the Russian nesting dolls, or *matryoshkas*, where each doll has an unknown number of smaller dolls encased within it. Consider your own healing as a careful and curious cracking open of each figurine, from the outside in. With every minor shift, with every choice to open yourself to what could lie within, with each *aha* moment, you can uncover an entire layer of emotional or mental experience that wasn't recognized or accepted by you before. It's challenging. It can be painful. But it's vital for a healthy life.

Kate Fagan, quoted above, recently wrote about college track athlete Maddy Holleran, who tragically leaped from a nine-story garage to her death, literally running away from her life, due to what now appears to be intense hopelessness and despair. Although she had a loving family who knew she was struggling to some extent, the real Maddy was buried beneath layers of intense pressure and smiling selfies. No one recognized the complexity of her struggle. Even her suicide was carefully planned and executed, with thoughtful gifts arranged for her loved ones. Maddy wasn't aware that she didn't have to feel trapped in her perfect-looking life. She didn't know that it was possible to discover what was hurting her so badly and why she was lost.

Let's talk about this process of discovery. Hopefully, a story from Oprah Winfrey can be helpful. She writes, "I realize now that even though I have had the kind of career that brings with it an element of power, versions of my childhood abuser continually showed up in my life disguised in other forms... I allowed abusers to cross boundaries rather than confronting them. My childhood history of physical and sexual abuse conditioned me to be silent... I pushed those feelings down with food" (2017, 126).

She goes on to talk about her own *aha* moment. One day she was visiting her father. She'd already achieved immense success in her life, yet she found herself submissively taking orders from one of her past molesters for over-easy eggs. She was shocked by her speechlessness. "Looking back, this was a seminal moment for me. I reverted to the silence of my nine-year-old girl self, who thought that speaking up would cause me to be blamed... Making that connection feels like a light bulb has finally been switched on. *Aha! Not only have I broken open, I've broken through!*" (2017, 126–127).

It was in that moment that Oprah understood that she was still living by the survival strategy she'd used as a child—to be silent, to be invisible. All her popularity and the respect that she had in her world wasn't enough for her to stand her ground, to refuse her abuser. She recognized that her emotional freedom was still being held hostage by her past, and she could so clearly see the tentacles of her abuse still strangling her in the present. Not only was her strategy no longer needed or wanted, it now was hurtful to her. She could change it. But awareness had to come first.

### Reflection 21: What Scares Me About Digging Deeper?

How did you respond to Maddy's story and where "looking perfect" could lead? What was it like to read Oprah's story? What did it spark in you? Maddy's story is tragic; Oprah's, more hopeful. Both stress that things you might not be able to easily see—or struggle to admit—can heavily influence your life. What would get in your way of searching for what might be under the surface of your own life? What scares you about digging a little deeper? Please take a moment to write your answers in your journal.

Often, when someone is ready to leave therapeutic treatment, they'll jokingly say something like, "Yay! I'm healed." Hopefully, they've discovered the beauty and freedom of being in the present moment and being their true self. That process is far from over, but they're sensing they're ready to fly on their own. They've broadened both their understanding and their skill set.

Change, growth, and healing are processes—they're journeys, not destinations. Your vulnerabilities, whatever they are, will come around to haunt you every now and then, even after the good work you've done in this book or with a therapist. Situations will trigger old wounds. Irrationalities in your thinking will seep back in— maybe due to fatigue, maybe due to you not paying attention or catching yourself. It's not that healing never occurred or that your own previous insight and change wasn't real. But in your humanity, in your imperfection, you may tend to slip back into an old survival strategy. Even Oprah won't catch every time she falls into the pattern that she recognized in that light bulb moment.

Earlier, I stated (alluding to a quote by Andrew Solomon), "If the opposite of depression is vitality, the opposite of perfectly hidden depression is self-acceptance." I want to stress this again. And here's my reason: Healing in perfectly hidden depression requires acceptance that your vulnerabilities, your weaknesses, and your faults are all vital and acceptable parts of you. That is a huge part of the healing work. There is no shame in having them. They do not suggest failure. You have them because you're human. You're a result of your experience. Through acceptance you can change, because acceptance is far from resignation or giving up.

Self-acceptance brings freedom.

The work of perfectly hidden depression leads inward mentally and especially emotionally. Rather than trying to reengage outwardly, the goal is to allow and let go—to see the constrictions of your existence and confront some of the rules you're telling yourself you have to follow—and to deeply feel the change that begins to occur as you do.

There have been far too many Maddys. My hope is that this work leads you far away from that devastating potential.

### Reflection 22: What Discoveries Have I Made So Far? What Challenges Do I Need to Give Myself?

Take a little time to go through your journal at this juncture. Go back to the beginning and remember how you felt when you first began to write down your actual thoughts and feelings. See how you've progressed and changed. What did you think you'd never write that you did? Or are you still struggling to allow your own discovery?

Many perfectionistic people find it hard to write because they're evaluating as they go, trying to sound "good." If you've struggled in this way, know that it's normal. But it's also something to try to tweak as you go further. Challenge yourself to go deeper. Risk writing something that you never thought you could. Or if you don't want to write it down, simply say the words aloud. Perhaps "I hated my mom" or "I feel so lonely sometimes I feel like I'm going to break apart." Let the words go. And breathe through the emotion that comes with it.

Remember, tears are about intensity, not weakness. Whether you cry because you're mad, cry because you're joyful, or cry because you're sad, your tears reflect the depth of the feeling or perhaps the sensitivity you have to a certain issue. If tears flow, let them flow. And continue patting yourself on the back for work well done.

## The Five C's in the Healing Process

Let's talk briefly about each of the five stages of healing for perfectly hidden depression: consciousness, commitment, confrontation, connection, and change. And for a visual, refer to the book's introduction to see the five stages of healing diagram.

**Consciousness.** The first stage is about developing an awareness and acceptance that something is a problem. Although part of every healing process, this stage is more complicated for you because you've convinced yourself (or at least had done so before beginning to read) that all ten characteristics of perfectly hidden depression—from perfectionism to denial of most emotional pain—are normal. You seem fantastic to others. You're not crying or emotionally unstable. What could be the problem?

The problem, as the more aware part of you knows, is that you're living a hoax, and it's creating tremendous loneliness and emptiness inside of you. So, your first step is to become conscious of the everyday damage of this syndrome—how it keeps you isolated and unknown.

**Commitment.** The second stage can be complex. Why is this? Because commitment involves letting go of control. And your fear of ambiguity, of not staying in total control, of not knowing what your new life might look like has kept your pain—your anger, your sadness—under wraps. Accepting this ambiguity may bring actual terror and cause you to vacillate: *Is this actually a good idea? Or do I need to stop now?*

Yet if you stay committed and begin to experience the tight ropes around your actions and life loosening, as you begin to breathe more freely, hope will arrive. And hope is where you'll find the courage to stay committed.

**Confrontation.** The third stage deals with sorting out the rules and beliefs that have governed your life, deciding which ones still fit and which need to be released.

**Connection.** The fourth stage occurs when you feel the emotion that will come as a result of releasing the rules and beliefs that no longer serve you. Confrontation and Connection are closely interwoven, and interactions between these two stages can happen quickly, bouncing back and forth like a ping-pong ball.

**Change.** The final stage brings real risk but also freedom, spontaneity, and being in the present—all things that have eluded you to a great extent so far in your life. But now is the time for you to move toward new self-expression and be the wonderfully imperfect human being that you are!

# Attain Consciousness

## *"How Could I Be Depressed?*
## *My Life Looks Perfect"*

*"E. L. Doctorow once said that 'writing a novel is like driving a car at night. You can only see as far as your headlights, but you can make the whole trip that way.' You don't have to see where you're going or everything that you will pass along the way. You just have to see two or three feet ahead of you. This is right up there with the best advice about writing, or life, I have ever heard."*

—Anne Lamott, author of Bird by Bird

As soon as you began reading this book, you started working on the first step of healing: Consciousness. It's a must in any therapeutic change. You must identify a problem as a problem before you can change it. You've begun to understand that perfectly hidden depression exists and has had a painful impact on you and your relationships. Simply after reading the first few chapters of this book, you're realizing how you've kept secret your true experience of life for years, creating instead a persona that looks good to others and has served to help you feel safe.

But right now, you're like a turtle when it senses danger. Your automatic strategy is to hide any vulnerability within a shell of perfectionism. You abruptly pull any sign of it in and hold on like your life depends on it.

So how do you begin to change what may seem automatic?

The first step is to become more conscious of yourself and your reactions. And it takes lots of practice—I'll say this frequently. These are huge mental and emotional shifts.

Let's talk about two components of consciousness that are intertwined with one another: *awareness* and *mindfulness*.

## Awareness and Gaining Knowledge

You now have the knowledge of how the ten characteristics act together to create a syndrome that can be paralyzing and destructive. But before reading this book, you could've been more or less aware of your actions. There are three different levels of awareness that could have existed.

The first level is *total awareness*. Hiding behaviors may have been intentional for quite some time. You may know when they started, how they started, or why they started. And you made a conscious choice every day to keep your own troubles invisible. This may sound similar to popular literature's "smiling depression" or "high-functioning depression." Yet people who identify with these two terms talk about being depressed. They've admitted it freely. They may have sought treatment for it. Even on this level of awareness of perfectly hidden depression, you've likely not recognized yourself as depressed. Something caused you to need to protect yourself. And a perfect-looking facade became the way you accomplished that feat.

The second level is *lack of awareness*. Your hiding became so entrenched that it became unconscious. It became your identity. Let's talk for a minute about what is meant by "unconscious."

A traumatic memory, emotion, idea, or extremely painful experience can be stored in the part of the mind that is unknown to you.

It's not as if you knew it existed but weren't thinking about it. That's what "subconscious" is—like forgetting today is your birthday. Your mind has the power to place something extremely far away from your awareness in order to protect you. And it becomes unconscious. The characteristics of perfectly hidden depression, as well as what originated them, then cannot easily be recognized. Some say that therapy itself is creating an environment where what is unconscious can become conscious.

Rebecca told me, "Before I read about PHD, I'd never have thought of myself as depressed. Ever. If I even wondered, if I listened to my gut that knew something was wrong, I'd feel incredible shame, like I didn't appreciate the good things in my life. I can't even imagine allowing myself to think or say some of the things I've said to you since we've been working together. I didn't even realize how I was living. Or not living."

Rebecca was making what had been unconscious conscious.

The third level is a more *mixed bag*. Some of the ten characteristics were known and quite intentional. Others were more surprising when you realized their place as part of the syndrome and you, again, hadn't been conscious of them.

Why are these levels important? Answer: Because I don't want you to make the mistake that being aware of how you coped makes you less worthy of compassion. Even if you "knew what you were doing," you need to develop empathy for the pain you were trying to handle. And if you didn't "know what you were doing," there's no reason to shame yourself. You're going to understand more and more the "why" of this particular coping strategy as the healing process continues. Whether you were aware all along, or you're just beginning to become aware, you can accept where you are now and go forward.

### Reflection 23: How Aware Have I Been of Hiding?

Which level of awareness have you had? If the first—total awareness—write out what it's felt like to be so intentional in your hiding, as well as what it's felt like to keep the pressure on, day after day.

If you identify with the second level—being unconscious of what you were doing—what's it like for you to begin to become more aware? Does it feel like you're putting the puzzle pieces together? Or is there a part of you that wants to find fault with the whole idea of perfectly hidden depression?

If the third level—the mixed bag—describs you, has it been confusing to know some choices have been very intentional while others seemed more under the surface? Which areas were you aware of and which seemed like your natural way of being?

### Overcoming Denial

No matter what type you identify with, you likely deny the extent of the damage that your perfectionism has created—unless you've become terribly despairing or even suicidal. Denial is the opposite of awareness. And you've been in a heap of denial.

Many of the ten characteristics of perfectly hidden depression are woven into the fabric of your being. In fact, even considering changing them may be difficult to accept.

For example, if you identify with the first characteristic—perfectionism with a constant, shaming critical voice—you've likely labeled it as helpful, not as toxic to your functioning. Your reputation is built on it. You're seen as a go-to, get-it-done, hardworking person. Why would you change that?

You might think, "Yes, I can be hard on myself. But I count on my perfectionism to keep the quality of my work where I need it to be." That's not a healthy you talking. That's denial talking.

### Emotional Responses to Your Denial

As you begin to confront your own denial, you may have different emotional responses to reading that your arsenal of choices may not act in your best interest.

First, you may welcome the information. It may feel like relief. It fits with the gut feeling you've had for a long time, which is that something's wrong that you haven't been able to put your finger on. It's as if someone has handed you the last remaining pieces of a puzzle—and now you can see the entire picture. The label "perfectly hidden depression" gives what you've been experiencing a name—a tangible identity. It can offer a lens through which you can discover and understand what's been happening in your mind and heart. It's important for you now to get the facts, so that you can assess what direction you want to go. You're taking the bull by the horns. You're eager to pick denial apart when it tries to convince you that perfectionism isn't a problem.

Second, you may feel overwhelmed. It's hard work, and you might fight the tendency to put down this book and avoid any more thoughts about perfectly hidden depression. Denial can feel much easier than awareness. It can feel like too much to consider changing. You don't want any more information. Enough is enough. And you may stay stuck in the syndrome, not being able to believe that healing is actually possible. I hope this doesn't happen. But if it does, please know that there's a time for everything. Please don't put off looking at your perfectly hidden depression too long.

Third, you may struggle with fear and worry, especially that you'll be labeled as less than or incompetent if anyone finds out. This is normal, given the stigma in our culture and world regarding mental and emotional issues. If you've judged others' vulnerability as weakness or frailty (refer to what you wrote in Reflection 14, What Are My Feelings About Mental Illness, Really?), then trying to accept your own mental and emotional struggles can be tricky. Even if you've shown compassion to others, no matter whether their struggles were largely mental or emotional, you may still have trouble directing that compassion toward yourself. At the risk of sounding like a broken record, you're accustomed to a fairly rigid way of living your life—and moving forward can be scary.

At every step, we'll deal with this fear, but especially in the next chapter: Commitment. You'll know when you're winning the battle with fear. You'll recognize that there's no going back—and that you don't want to hide from how your heart and your mind are responding.

## Mindfulness

The second component of consciousness is *mindfulness*. Whereas awareness can happen in an instant, giving fresh information, mindfulness deepens your experience of the present. The authors of *The Mindful Way Through Depression: Freeing Yourself from Chronic Unhappiness* write that "*mindfulness* is much more than paying attention more thoroughly. It is paying attention *differently*—changing *how* we pay attention… Being mindful means intentionally turning off the autopilot mode in which we operate so much of the time—brooding about the past, for instance, or worrying about the future—and instead tuning in to things as they are in the present with full awareness" (Williams et al. 2007, 54).

Mindfulness is taking awareness to the next level and practicing how to stay very centered in exactly what this moment has to offer. It's a huge field in and of itself. Whereas anxiety tends to keep you thinking about the future—and depression typically keeps you focused on the past—mindfulness accentuates the importance and energy of the now. And as Anne Lamott's opening quote suggests, you can travel all of life's journey only being able to see what's a few feet in front of you—what's in the present.

But the practice of mindfulness has another, vital function. Mindfulness practitioners teach that if you simply notice and accept an emotion or a thought in the present, but you don't fuel it in any way, that very acceptance can disempower it. It's what we think about or believe about something that causes us to make a judgment about it—not the thing itself.

Let me offer myself as an example. I've been very open about having anxiety—to be specific, a panic disorder. I'm a student of mindfulness with much still to learn. But I've been trying to be more mindful—to simply notice my anxiety but stay in the present and allow it to be, rather than hating it or fueling it with fear. My particular panic causes my legs to shake. The other day, in a crowded, hot boutique, the shaking began to happen. I could feel adrenaline start to make my heart beat faster. Instead of freaking out, feeding the panic with the thought, *I bet this is going to lead into a big panic attack,* I simply noticed my legs. I said to myself, *Hmm… it feels like my legs are starting to shake.* I didn't heap fear or shame on it. And the panic, as well as its symptoms, slowly faded away.

Mindfulness attends to the present. It doesn't focus on what just happened, or what's going to happen, but what *is* happening. Right now. Like anything else you practice, the more you practice staying in the moment, the sooner it can become a new pattern, a new behavior, and a ready option for you.

### Mindfulness and PHD

So what about mindfulness is specifically important for perfectly hidden depression?

Mindfulness is key in experiencing full emotional expression. And you have great trouble expressing your emotional states. Anger, sadness, disappointment, despair, and even true joy stay at bay because strong emotions might lead you to feel out of control. However, sitting with emotions, being mindful of them, gives them space in the present. The feeling can emerge very slowly. Or it can erupt into the moment. But you learn to manage it, to allow it. Emotions that you believed intolerable can be felt and released. The voice of your perfectly hidden depression has told you quite the opposite—that if you felt pain, it might never go away.

Think of emotions as waves in an ocean. Each feeling—each wave—has a life of its own. It begins far out, deep in the sea itself. Then gradually as it rolls to shore, you become aware of its shape, its strength, its power. But when its time is done, when it disappears into froth on the beach, it's replaced by the next emotion wave. You can feel the undertow reflecting its muted energy under the surface once again. This process goes on and on and on. Mindfulness is being aware of each moment of an emotion wave's apparent life, riding it until it inevitably comes to an end.

This doesn't mean that staying mindful or allowing emotions to emerge is a smooth, effortless process. It can be frightening and very intense. If it gets too intense, or if for any reason you don't feel safe, then it's time to ask for professional help.

Let's start with a simple mindfulness practice. All you'll be doing is sitting with your feelings.

### Reflection 24: Mindful Focusing on the Breath

Sit somewhere very comfortable in whatever position feels good. Set a timer for five minutes. Breathe deeply, close your eyes, focus on your breathing, and be still. Try staying focused on your breath. Don't judge the experience or think too much about it. If your mind wanders, bring it back gently to focus on the breath. You can count your breaths if that is helpful for your focus.

When the timer goes off, take another minute or two to see what emotions might be there, like watching the wave of emotion dissipate. You may feel relieved, or you may be frustrated because you're having a hard time. Open your eyes and write about your experience. Good for you!

Now let's read about Danielle's very difficult journey to be in the moment.

*Danielle's Story:* Stepping into the Moment

*Danielle had been sexually abused as a toddler by a cousin who still lives in her childhood home with her parents. She'd confronted her cousin and told her parents and siblings about what had happened. They listened, but nothing changed. Her cousin denied everything.*

*Now, as an adult, Danielle was struggling with perfectly hidden depression, post-traumatic stress disorder, obsessive-compulsive disorder, and anorexia. Her anorexia had become so severe that she had to be hospitalized and normalize her eating before we could continue treatment. She didn't like that and fought the idea. But with the support of her husband, she agreed to go. After she returned, a nutritionist was brought in, so her work on her trauma and perfectionism could safely continue.*

*She always had a smile on her face during therapy, no matter the topic, and would catch any tear before it rolled down*

*her check, highly uncomfortable that her pain was showing.
As therapy became more and more specific about her abuse and
her family's avoidance and denial, she would obsessively clean
her home to avoid feelings that were growing more insistent as
she and I talked and processed. And she had to very carefully
monitor her eating and exercise—a battle that she didn't always
win. Her progress was slow. But proceeding safely was
paramount.*

*When painful feelings grew more insistent, one day she said,
"I need to sit with these feelings. I don't want to. I'm afraid of
them. But I'm not making good decisions. I don't want to eat.
I'm cleaning too much, I work out too hard, even to the point of
hurting myself. I feel invisible in my family and even to myself."*

*So she and I sat. She allowed her feelings to surface without
judgment. Without censorship. Without shame. She had so much
to grieve. Slowly the tears came. Sobs followed. And I simply
held her.*

*When Danielle became mindful, when she stayed in the
present and allowed emotions to surface, she found relief.
After years of hiding, she could let go.*

Feeling pain deeply isn't pleasant. It hurts. It feels extremely vulnerable. Feeling joy can be amazing. But it too passes. Emotions come and go. Yet they are markers of what has been important—what has shaped you, for better or for worse. Danielle went on from that session and was ready to make other significant changes, in being able to both share more and address the deeper levels of her fears. You're already starting to do that.

Remember, mindfulness is connecting to the present. The technique supports "being" instead of "doing." Mindfulness begins first with being aware. When an emotion rises, you say, "I'm aware that I'm sad." "I'm aware that I feel lonely." "I'm aware that I feel relief." Almost like a light that you can barely detect in the distance, you can choose to go toward that light. And as you safely move toward the feeling, you'll deepen your experience of it.

**Reflection 25:** Practicing Mindfulness

You can be mindful at any point—be aware of how your body feels sitting in a chair, or slow down and savor the food you're eating. Meditation is simply a practice of a certain type of focus. There are multiple mindfulness and meditation apps available—Headspace, Calm, and 10% Happier among them—that will help you conquer whatever self-consciousness you might have, as well as what mindfulness folks call "monkey mind"—our minds jumping all over the place!

Jon Kabat-Zinn, quoted in this book and a noted expert in the field, has meditation and mindfulness exercises on diverse topics and of various lengths on his website. Please go check out one of these and begin practicing. You'll gain confidence in your ability to work with your mind in this way. Practice will help you get better—but perfection isn't achievable.

We'll use this practice of mindfulness throughout the following chapters. In the next chapter, we'll talk about the Commitment stage. It's one of the chief issues in your work with perfectly hidden depression, and we'll discuss the potential pros and cons of going forward with the risk.

# Make the Commitment

## *"I'm Scared to Be Any Different... What If I Fail?"*

*Haw looked down the dark passageway and was aware of his fear. What lay ahead? Was it empty? Or worse, were there dangers lurking? He began to imagine all kinds of frightening things that could happen to him. He was scaring himself to death.*

*Then he laughed at himself. He realized his fears were making it worse. So he did what he would do if he wasn't afraid. He moved in a new direction.*

—Spencer Johnson, author of *Who Moved My Cheese?*

Commitment involves a promise or an agreement between you and someone or something else—commitment to marriage, commitment to a job or a cause, commitment to your kids. It's something that's important to you. It matters enough that you feel an extra responsibility or push to engage fully, to feel deeply connected, to be willing to give the time and effort it takes to honor that commitment.

Your work on perfectly hidden depression is a commitment to yourself.

So, let's begin this chapter with a reflection.

**Reflection 26:** Considering Commitment

By now, you're good at taking the time to do these reflections. You've been committed! Let's look at other things you've felt committed to in your lifetime.

List the ideas, organizations, beliefs, people, or causes that you've felt committed to through the years. They may have stayed largely the same, or they may have changed a great deal. Write about what you've learned through those commitments. Not all commitments work out well. Others do. Do any of those commitments get in the way of your own self-care?

What helps you stick with a commitment? What commitments have you let go? What makes you ready to commit to this work?

## Overcoming the Stumbling Blocks to Commitment

As we discussed in the previous chapter, denial can get in the way of awareness and mindfulness. It and the fear of stigma are two major stumbling blocks to the commitment to heal. What are some others that you might encounter along the way?

Here are five that are strongly linked with perfectionism:

- Having such a rigid commitment that you'll shame yourself and quit if you falter

- Beginning with a goal that's too hard

- Going it alone and not asking for what you need along the way

- Dealing with the fear of giving up familiar coping strategies while stress increases

- Other mental illnesses growing worse due to fear and stress

Let's talk about specific strategies for how you can prevent getting waylaid by these stumbling blocks.

## Redefining a Rigid Commitment as Intention

In order to heal, your behaviors need to change. But if commitment to change becomes another thing to do perfectly, you're much more likely to quit the whole process if you make a mistake or run into difficulty. To help with this, let's redefine "commitment" as "intention."

*Commitment* involves a pledge or promise and a sense of duty. It can easily grow into a rigid measure of success or failure, as with the thought, *I've made this commitment and I'm sticking to it.*

*Intention* is an aim or a purpose but is innately more flexible. Intention brings with it a sense of soft focus. It's a choice to commit— but with a little wiggle room. You can absorb fresh information along the way and determine if your intention needs to change.

Dan Siegel, in his book *Aware: The Science and Practice of Presence*, discusses what changes occur when what he terms "kind intention" is your focus. "Intention primes the mind for maliciousness or for kindness, and shapes the inner life of our body and the inter life of our relationships… *How intention glows determines where attention goes, neural firing flows, and neural and interpersonal connection grow*" (2018, 96–97).

We don't want to delve too deeply into the neurobiology or the philosophy of all this. I, for one, might get lost. However, it's interesting to think about how you've responded to past commitments. What did your journaling help you see? Did a commitment morph into an inflexible duty? Did you quit (or hide) because you weren't perfect?

Duty isn't bad in and of itself, don't get me wrong. Commitment is solidly based on what you value. And values define us as either similar to or different from others. Yet since perfectionism is such an ingrained trait in you, you need to consider not only *what* you want to change in yourself but also *how* you want to change it. And that's done with kindness.

If you have an intention to do something and you don't succeed, you may feel guilt (the behavior is "bad") rather than shame (the self is "bad"). However, it's tricky. Perfectionists like you can even turn failed intentions into fodder for self-loathing.

I've struggled with perfectionism all my life. And it can invade even the most random thoughts or actions. Here's an example. Late in the afternoon one day, I remembered that I'd wanted (I'd had the intention) to call a friend who was going through something very difficult. I'd seen patients all day and, frankly, forgot. Out rushed my own scorn and self-chastising. This happened so quickly that I barely recognized when my critical voice had taken over. (Remember those gremlins?) But I caught it just in time. "Hold on, Bob," I said. (Remember the name of your critical voice? Mine is Bob.) "I'll jot it down and make sure I do it tomorrow. I like being someone who would want to reach out in the first place. I'm going to continue trying to be thoughtful. So be quiet!"

Hopefully, you hear the kindness I directed at myself when I told Bob to simmer down. I had the intention to make contact. I'm human and forgot. The non-perfectionistic thing to do is to allow my disappointment to increase my intention to get it done tomorrow, not allow shame to chew me up and spit me out.

What's the major concern here? It's quitting if you falter—if you make a mistake or forget or simply lose your resolve for a bit—because then you're besieged with shame. It's inevitable that you're going to fall back into perfectionistic behavior. You're going to struggle to express your feelings sometimes, much less be mindful of them. I've listened to many people who identify with perfectly hidden depression say, "I hate that it's taking me so long to get this. We've been working on this for weeks." It will take time and patience—lots of patience—and *kindness* toward yourself.

Remember, this isn't something else you have to do perfectly.

### Reflection 27: Checking in with My Intention and Commitment

Write freely about how you're processing this idea of intention versus commitment. Some of you may be bristling with thoughts like, *What is she saying? That commitment is a bad thing? Commitment reflects my values and I'm not giving that up.* If you need to, write about that and see what it brings. Since you struggle with such a strong sense of responsibility, it may be hard for you to adopt a kinder, more flexible attitude.

Name what you believe you're committed to and what you have intentions about. How are the two different from one another? How do you react if you don't or can't follow through with a commitment from time to time? How is that tied in with your perfectionism?

What would it feel like to be kinder to yourself? If you say something shameful to yourself, what would you rather say? Take a moment to be mindful of the feelings these considerations have brought you.

### Begin with the Simplest Goal

Because you're a perfectionist, you might have the urge to start with the most challenging goal you can think of. But when anyone begins a process of change, it's usually not a great idea to set the hardest goal first. You want to take small steps that you can more easily accomplish and that will build confidence as you test out a more imperfect, vulnerable self. Remember, you want to set yourself up for success and hope.

To help you set a goal, please turn back in your journal to your answers from Reflection 12, in which you identified the ten characteristics of PHD that you've most relied upon. Find the characteristic that you ranked a 1. (If you ranked "accompanying mental health issues" as a 1, please skip over that and go to the characteristic you ranked a 2; we'll talk about other disorders later in this section.)

Now let yourself think of an intention you could set to tweak that characteristic a bit. For example, if it's counting your blessings constantly so that you don't "feel sorry for yourself," begin to play with the idea of how you might challenge that habit.

For now, just visualize yourself making the change. Sit with it. Pay attention to what happens emotionally as you imagine setting your intention and following through.

### Reflection 28: Carrying Out Goals

In this reflection, you'll want to clearly identify the characteristic you've chosen as the simplest to change, along with its replacement behavior. For example, if focusing on the well-being of others but not allowing them into your inner world is the characteristic you want to change, then your replacement behavior might be to allow others in on something that has disappointed or saddened you.

Your goal is to be vulnerable. Following this idea, you could text a friend to see if she can meet for a cup of coffee, with the intention of telling her about reading this book. If you struggle or can't "make" yourself risk being vulnerable as of yet, no worries. But at least go in with that intention. Remember the whole "Rome wasn't built a day" thing. Be patient and persistent. You'll get there in your own time. Good luck!

## Ask for What You Need

You've lived much of your life rarely, if ever, asking for help. Going it alone is something you're quite accustomed to doing. You've worked hard to be seen as self-sufficient, the problem solver in a group, or the person who can take charge and get things done. You trust in your ability to help others. Your perfectionistic drive has led you to hide whatever problems might arise, especially those problems associated with feeling confused or lost. The fact that you picked up this book at all is a minor miracle. Even accepting help from this book may feel like you're failing somehow.

But going it alone is another major stumbling block to your healing. You're struggling with perfectly hidden depression in part because you haven't asked safe, supportive people for what you need. Now is the time to build a support network.

Beginning to cope with whatever trauma might be in your past is *very* difficult work. You may even cringe when you read the word "trauma." You might think, *I wouldn't call it that. That's too dramatic for what happened to me.* But keep in mind that you've discounted your pain for years—and it isn't easy to stop. I've included the stories of others who've covered up their true selves in order to address this tendency to discount what happened in your life. When you read their stories, do you recognize their pain? Loss? Unexpressed grief? I bet you do. That's trauma! Please hold that same yardstick up to yourself.

Let me share with you an experience I had a couple of years ago, keeping in mind my own perfectionistic bent.

### *Margaret's Story:* Finding an Exit

*I was visiting a residential psychiatric center with a group of therapists. The center wanted us to experience their program firsthand and participate in the activities and classes available to the patients. It was fascinating.*

*The first night, after dinner, we were led in front of two huge closed doors. We were told we were going to be led into a maze with only one exit. We were assured there was an exit, and it was our job to find it. We were then blindfolded and led by someone else into the room. My hand was put on what felt like a rope. There were some rules: You weren't allowed to release the rope or go underneath it. You followed the rope until you discovered the exit. We were asked to be totally silent. If you thought you'd found the exit, or if you needed something, you could raise your other hand and wait for someone to come to you.*

*Soft music was playing in the background. We clumsily bumped into one another, nervous laughter filtering through the room. I traveled around for what felt like forever, trying to envision a pattern in my mind of where I was going and where I'd been. I could find no exit. I held up my hand, thinking I'd brilliantly figured it out.*

*"Is the exit letting go?" I asked, thinking that breaking the rules might be the way out.*

*"No."*

*I tried again, becoming restless and irritated with myself, as a growing crowd that had found the "exit" were quietly talking with one another.*

*I raised my hand again. "Is the answer that there's no exit?"*

*"No, Margaret, keep traveling."*

*I was getting more and more agitated and emotional. This was embarrassing. And suddenly I stopped. I knew. I raised my hand for the last time.*

*I whispered with tears in my eyes, "I need to ask for help."*

*That was the exit: admitting that I needed help. It was so simple, yet very difficult to allow myself to see. I'd been so purposeful, so fixed on my own ego getting affirmed, my own mind solving the problem, that the simple answer of asking others for what I needed was ignored. It was quite the lesson, not only for me as a therapist but also for me as a person. It was extremely moving and led me to open myself even more to others that weekend.*

We all need help. You're not here to do it on your own. The experiences of others who have identified with perfectly hidden depression are sprinkled throughout these pages to help you. One day, you'll help someone else.

### Reflection 29: The Maze of Life

Turn to your journal again and write about how you think you might have experienced the maze. Have you ever been in one? If so, did you experience anxiety? What do you think it would've been like to watch others struggle with the answer?

More generally, how good are you at asking for help? Maybe you can, maybe not. Try to think and write about several times when, in hindsight, you could've asked for help and didn't. What stopped you? What would you like to believe about asking for help now?

Asking for what you need is one thing. But what would it be like to share your healing journey with one trusted person? Having someone to talk with, to bounce ideas off of, to seek reassurance from, and to ask help from can be vital for your commitment and intention to thrive. You may not be ready. That's okay if you're not, but I want you to gently consider its importance. Going it alone is definitely something you'll want to change. And if you begin to practice, a little at a time, you'll learn how to engage more fully and feel more connected with others.

It's not important with whom you begin your journey but that, at your own pace, you begin. You can start by looking at someone in your inner circle. Or you may decide to start with someone who you know is a confidential source of guidance and support, such as a therapist.

## Balance Change with Stability

During the entire process of challenging and changing the familiar patterns of perfectionism and perfectly hidden depression, you have to discover a safe balance between desired change and a need for stability. Think about the old game of pick-up sticks, or the more recent one, Jenga. The strategy to win involves a careful assessment of what stick or what Jenga piece you can remove without the entire thing crashing down.

Someone with perfectly hidden depression faces this very challenge. You decide where to begin the change and, slowly and with compassion for yourself, take down the persona, piece by piece, and replace it with a healthier, more open, and more vulnerable self. You don't want to go too fast: again, these behaviors have served a purpose. And when you begin to alter them, you're likely to feel the emotions or remember the painful memories they've been covering up.

Let's talk briefly about Laura. She's a great example of the process of beginning to change new behaviors and what you can uncover when you do.

### *Laura's Story:* The Aftermath of Positive Change

*Laura was a fiftysomething woman who'd been in an emotionally abusive relationship for years. She'd taken the blame over and over for the conflicts between her and her husband in order to keep the peace. She focused on raising her kids, volunteering for several organizations in the community, and running an interior design firm that specialized in remodeling. She often did pro bono work for those who couldn't afford her services and was known citywide for her generosity.*

*She'd chosen to challenge her habit of taking on excessive responsibility as the best place for her healing work to begin. She laughed, "It may not be much, but I went to my PEO meeting this month. They were asking for volunteers to run the upcoming silent auction—to ask for items and get them all ready. I sat on my hands. Literally."*

*She then went on to discuss what had happened when she left the meeting. "I got in my car and, all of sudden, there were tears in my eyes. I felt ashamed. Other people are as busy as I am. I should've taken my share. Then I stopped myself. Why do I feel like I've always got to do more?"*

*The answer to that question became clear. Laura was adopted as a child, treasured and pampered by her parents. Yet they would also remind her how lucky she was—that if she hadn't been adopted by them, she wouldn't have all the privilege she enjoyed now. Her worth didn't reside in her—it was dependent on their generosity—or that was the message they doled out to her as a child. There was no arguing with that logic. Rationally, those facts were true. They'd adopted her. But she'd thanked her parents over and over for the adoption.*

*It was in that moment that Laura began to recognize that her need to invest inexhaustible energy in others was based on the insecurity she'd felt as a child. She finally saw that she had nothing to prove. She was deserving of love. Simply sitting on her hands had opened the way to incredible insight and self-compassion.*

These kinds of connections are highly likely to happen as you continue this journey. We'll talk later about how to build those new revelations and connections, and cope with the pain of them. For now, let's talk about a couple of possible "hitches" along the way as you balance your desire to change with the need to remain stable. First, we'll touch on your tendency to discount small but highly significant steps. Second, we'll look at how you may feel worse before you feel better—a common process in any change.

### Acknowledge Small but Vital Changes

I've said this before, and I'll say it again: you're a perfectionist, and small changes can easily be demeaned as not a big deal. This only leads to shame, which is likely to stop you in your tracks. Please don't minimize the work you're doing. Instead, acknowledge the changes you're making as significant, no matter how "small" they seem to you.

Did you notice how Laura discounted her new, quite remarkable behavior by saying, "It may not be much…"? This attitude can derail your commitment and intention, so please watch for this tendency. Again, these beginning risks are huge for someone with perfectly hidden depression. Think of them as building blocks for "rebuilding" how you think of yourself and how you allow others to see you.

## Reflection 30: What Revelations Have Emerged for You Since Beginning the Book?

Please go back to Reflection 9, Taking Stock of What's in My Emotion Closet, and reread what you wrote. I still don't want you to get out any box as of yet, but I'd like you to ask yourself, *Are there boxes that I can see now that I couldn't see when I began this book?* Or, *Would I change what I drew in this exercise now?*

You don't have to erase or change any box. Simply write down or draw a newer version in your journal now. It may show a difference between where you are now and where you were then. If it hasn't changed, then that's okay as well.

### Realize You May Feel Worse Before You Feel Better

It's fairly common in therapy for me to hear, "I feel worse than when I walked through your door." While this doesn't sound like a resounding endorsement of therapy or my own services, it reflects how change occurs. When you're stirring the emotional pot and gently challenging familiar belief systems, it's stressful. You're choosing to give up tight control over yourself. You can experience discomfort, agitation, and confusion. What you thought you knew, you don't know. What you felt about your life and your choices, you now question. It can all be disturbing for a while.

Some people quit therapy at this juncture, because the stress is simply too much. That's where they are in their lives, and I try to honor and support that when it occurs. But feeling worse before you feel better is a normal part of the process.

Since this is your own journey, since you're trying to read and journal your way to a new way of being, feeling worse may seem very disappointing. Your partner or spouse might notice, "You don't seem like your chipper self. What's going on?"

The tendency at this point may be to pull out of the ring and return to what you know. Hopefully, this reflection will help steady your resolve and keep you moving forward, even if you feel crummy. Remember Haw from the beginning quote of this chapter? "So he did what he would do if he wasn't afraid. He moved in a new direction." It's okay to be afraid, but you don't want your fear to govern you.

### Reflection 31: Using My Mantra

The very first reflection you were asked to do was the creation of a mantra—words that would be meaningful to you and would help remind you of your new direction. Please revisit that mantra now.

With the information you've acquired, you might want to change it, or it might still work very well for you. Or perhaps you couldn't think of one at the time; hopefully one will come to you now. Either way, post your mantra on your bathroom mirror, on your desktop at work, on your smartphone—wherever you think it would serve as a helpful reminder of your overarching goal. This kind of self-affirmation can be useful to remind you of where you're going as you cope with what may be more short-term or immediate struggles.

### Address Other Mental Illnesses You May Have

As you may recall, one of the ten characteristics of perfectly hidden depression is the potential for accompanying mental disorders. Eating disorders, anxiety disorders, obsessive-compulsive disorders, and addictions can all have within them a component of control, fear of losing control, or the need to escape anxiety. And they could be affecting your intention to heal. Therefore, they definitely need to be addressed.

In the previous chapter, Danielle was a great example of how mental illness could worsen or become more intense while doing this work. If excessive worry, compulsions in OCD, restricted or otherwise unhealthy eating, or addictions are your go-to way of handling that stress, it will be even more difficult to maintain your stability. (As stated previously, if you're feeling increasingly unstable, please seek immediate professional help.)

If you've not sought treatment for a recognized mental disorder, or it's very active at the moment, then consider attending to that before you get more heavily into this work. You'll have to be very honest with yourself and determine if you're putting the cart before the horse in focusing on perfectly hidden depression. It's not that perfectionism can't be destructive and dangerous in and of itself. We've recognized that. But it's far better to begin therapeutic work, especially self-guided therapeutic work, when you're as emotionally and mentally stable as possible.

### Reflection 32: Taking Stock of My Stability

Please take a moment to consider where you are mentally and emotionally. Answer the following questions in your journal: Am I going through some kind of life crisis that needs my attention right now? If so, what is it and what do I have control over that might be effective in lessening its impact? What mental disorders do I experience?

If you aren't sure, please take some time to do your own research. (You can jump ahead to Chapter 4 if you'd like to read the criteria for some of these disorders.) Are you stable enough to continue with a self-guided journey? And if you recognize you have OCD, anxiety, or another illness, or an addiction, what warning signs do you need to identify to know if you're getting in over your head? When should you seek medical or mental health guidance?

Think again about Danielle's story. Her cleaning was getting out of hand. And her anorexia was worsening. Those were warning signs for her. If you're in treatment, talk with your doctor or therapist so that you can ensure your stability during your work on perfectly hidden depression.

In the next chapter, we'll discuss in detail the steps to tuning into your own thinking and challenging the beliefs that no longer fit the life you want to create. You're opening yourself up to who you can be. And that's more than exciting—it's awesome.

# Confront Your Rulebook

## *"I'm so Incredibly Hard on Myself"*

*We can as easily become a prisoner of so-called positive thinking as of negative thinking. It too can be confining, fragmented, inaccurate, illusory, and wrong.*

—Jon Kabat-Zinn, author of *Wherever You Go, There You Are*

In this stage, Confrontation, you'll use the skill of mindfulness as you grow in awareness of how rigidly you've followed certain rules. Think of it as living in a box. Rules that may have initially been necessary for your emotional survival—your "must do" and "never do" lists—have governed your life. They've created walls around you that have kept difficult emotions and memories out, while they've also kept you locked inside. Included in this third stage will be even more encouragement to be proactive, to put these ideas into play, and to begin to create a sense of choice in your life. The assignments may take more time and will need to be revisited as you expand your awareness, with each tweak of one creating change in the other. It's a big undertaking, so take a deep, cleansing breath, take out your journal, and let's get started.

**Reflection 33:** What Does It Feel Like to Be at This Point?

Take a few minutes to journal about what's going on with your mind and heart as you take this next step. Say out loud, "Today I'm going to begin to challenge the way I think." Now listen for the messages that your critical or self-doubting voice are whispering to you. Are they telling you, "This is too hard," or, "It will disrupt your life too much"?

Notice the fear or the anxiety and try to refrain from fueling it with emotion. Check in with your fears and write down a reasonable, rational response, such as, "Yes, it's hard. And I've done hard things before." Or, "It's likely to disrupt my life for a while, but I'm miserable the way I'm living now."

You might want to recite your mantra again as you move ahead.

As mentioned before, it's vital to remember that this stage is highly interwoven with your emotional states. It's hard to separate the mental from the emotional, but for the sake of this book, we'll attempt that task for clarity. The mental changes you'll make will likely create fresh emotions and feelings of instability. And those very emotions are important clues. For now, please jot down these new emotional reactions or responses in your journal.

## Confronting Your Rules and Beliefs

Let's talk about the difference between beliefs and rules. *Rules* govern conduct. *Beliefs* are something you accept as true. The two are interactive. Beliefs may define the rules you follow. Yet the rules you follow may limit or expand your beliefs. For example, you might have the rule "I always put a smile on my face, no matter what." It's connected with the belief that "People won't like me if I don't smile."

There are thousands of beliefs you could have that define your perfectly hidden depression. Yours will be unique to you and be born from your religion, your family, your culture, your mentors, your native country, your gender, your sexual orientation, your experiences, your traumas—whatever has influenced you to believe what you believe and perceive what you perceive.

My goal in this chapter is to help you identify whether a rule or belief is constructive and helpful. If your belief stands up to reevaluation and helps you lead a fulfilling life, then it's a keeper. If not, you'll learn to challenge it, realize what kind of hold it has over you, and begin to loosen that hold.

That's your work for this stage and for the rest of your life. If you do nothing else with this book other than challenging the beliefs that don't serve you well, then I'll be happy. This change is that important.

### Where Do You Want Your New Choices to Lead?

What will you want in your life if you're not following the distorted rules of perfectly hidden depression? You may not know right now where you're going with all of this. You know what you don't want anymore. But where exactly are your new beliefs supposed to be leading you? In which direction are you going? What road are you following that will lead you to not having to hide?

Try completing this statement: "As I change the rules that I'm living by, I want to move toward _____."

One of my own mantras is: "What you do is not as important as *that* you do." It's the process that's important—the journey and what you're learning as you go. Where you end up isn't as important as that you begin to experience yourself and life in a refreshed, fulfilling, and tolerant way.

Let's also not make the mistake of assuming that you'll breeze through all of this. Your old rules will come out of the woodwork, clamoring to get your attention. It may be that the very process of allowing them to surface will be difficult. Perhaps even questioning them will feel wrong or as if you're being disloyal to someone or something. We've discussed the hurdles you might encounter. Now you'll be reassessing the beliefs and rules that have protected you and have been your reality. Changing that now can feel risky and even frightening. Your mind may go blank when you try to come up with ideas.

This next reflection will offer a structure that will be helpful.

### Reflection 34: Where Am I Going and What Beliefs Do I Want to Challenge to Get There?

Here are ten directions to move toward—ten desired changes you may want to make—that coordinate with the ten characteristics of perfectly hidden depression. In the left column are examples of self-destructive beliefs that are likely to sound familiar. In the right column are examples that will serve you much better and are self-constructive. You can make these your own—change them into whatever specific situation applies to your life. Remember, the emphasis is on *moving toward*. The focus is on the journey, not the destination.

### Ten Directions to Move Toward

|  | Self-Destructive Beliefs | Self-Constructive Beliefs |
| --- | --- | --- |
| 1. I want to move toward loosening the grip of perfectionism. | *I must look competent in everything.* | *I can accept that I make mistakes.* |
|  | *I'm okay with anxiety but I can't admit depression.* | *I can admit that I feel depressed.* |
|  | *Shame keeps me in line.* | *Shame keeps me stuck.* |
|  | *I must keep the pressure on or I'll turn into a slug.* | *I don't have to push to accomplish.* |

|  | Self-Destructive Beliefs | Self-Constructive Beliefs |
|---|---|---|
| 2. I want to move toward allowing others to take the lead. | *I need to feel in charge.* | *I like being helpful and want to experience being part of a team.* |
|  | *I cannot disappoint others.* | *It's okay to say no.* |
| 3. I want to move toward tolerance of emotional pain. | *If I feel my pain, it will never stop.* | *I can learn to manage my emotional pain.* |
|  | *I don't do feelings and I like it that way.* | *I may fear feeling and I can confront my fear.* |
| 4. I want to move toward calm and away from the need to worry. | *My worry keeps the people I love safe.* | *My worry keeps me unavailable in the moment.* |
|  | *If I don't look in control, I will appear weak.* | *The more I try to look in control, the more lonely I am.* |
| 5. I want to move toward enriching my life with creativity and play. | *I cannot relax.* | *I want to learn to listen to my body and rest.* |
|  | *I like things with answers.* | *I want to learn more about my creativity.* |
|  | *I have to have something to do.* | *I want to learn to focus on the moment.* |
| 6. I want to move toward allowing others into my emotional world. | *Others would be burdened by my problems.* | *I can give others the chance to be a good listener.* |
|  | *My worth is in what I can do for others.* | *Healthy relationships include give and take.* |
|  | *Having the spotlight on me is selfish.* | *Being self-aware is different from being selfish.* |

|  | Self-Destructive Beliefs | Self-Constructive Beliefs |
|---|---|---|
| 7. I want to move toward self-compassion. | *What happened to me is nothing if I compare it to what other people have to deal with.* | *What happened to me is important.* |
|  | *The past is in the past.* | *I can feel the pain from the past. It's important. I'm important.* |
|  | *It only happened once.* | *I will honor what happened to me.* |
| 8. I want to move toward accepting and managing my health issues. | *My anxiety isn't out of control.* | *I can recognize the severity of my symptoms.* |
|  | *It's weak to seek therapy.* | *It's empowering to reach out and reveal.* |
| 9. I want to move toward seeing both the positive and the negative. | *I refuse to feel sorry for myself.* | *Every pro has a con, every gain a loss.* |
|  | *Positivity is the thing that keeps me sane.* | *Rigid positivity keeps me from feeling vulnerable. I want to choose vulnerability.* |
| 10. I want to move toward building vulnerability and intimacy in relationships. | *Real life isn't like what you see on TV.* | *Real life is messy. And that's okay.* |
|  | *It's not fair to change our relationship now.* | *All healthy relationships change and grow.* |

Please journal about what it was like to read these very affirming statements. Try repeating the self-constructive beliefs to yourself. What does that feel like? Are you aware of any shifts in your thinking? Revisit the statement from earlier in this chapter: "As I change the rules that I'm living by, I want to move toward _____." What's your answer now? Or how do you want to be able to answer the question in a week, a month, or a year?

## How to Identify a Belief as Rigid, Self-Limiting, and Destructive

There are plenty of books written by experts about *cognitive-behavioral therapy* (CBT) that outline the distinct irrational beliefs of depression. CBT, in its simplest version, states that emotions arise from what you tell yourself or what you believe about something. Change your negative or irrational self-talk—what you believe—and you'll change the emotions connected with those thoughts. A change in how you feel will then greatly influence your behavior and lead to healthier well-being.

The classic CBT guidebook is *The Feeling Good Handbook* by David D. Burns. Another is *Breaking the Patterns of Depression* by Michael Yapko. Both identify common distortions that lead to depression and recommend replacing them with what CBT terms "rational" thoughts and beliefs. This book doesn't need to re-create what's already been expertly researched and eloquently discussed. I recommend that you pick up a copy of either of these books and see what specific distortions might be occurring in your own thinking.

For our purposes, we'll combine concepts and techniques from CBT and *family systems therapy*. Family systems therapy, again very simply put, focuses on how your family of origin, the family you grew up in, affected you in the past and influences you in the present. Let's see what happens when we hold these mirrors up to perfectly hidden depression.

## How to Evaluate Your Beliefs

Let's now discover the four basic steps of evaluating your beliefs. Each step will have its own revelations and reflections.

### Step 1. Identify the Spoken and Unspoken Rules That Underlie Your Actions (or Lack of Action)

Rules often reside in what you were taught or what you decided for yourself is what you have to do to be okay. These include your emotional survival strategies. For example, you may have learned spoken rules such as, "You have to brush your teeth twice a day," and, "You have to be nice to your brother." Other rules were never uttered but rather "understood." One in my family was: "It's not okay to openly express anger." No one ever told me that precisely, but no one ever got mad at home. And if you did, you were sent to your room "until you can act nicely." I heard one argument between my mom and dad when I was about seven and was certain they were divorcing.

Your culture, your religion, your school environment—these are other places where you developed your beliefs and the rules that emerged from them. Beliefs about what you're supposed to do as a man or a woman, what rules you need to follow because of cultural mores—all of that can be explored. And remember, some of those beliefs and rules were positive and helpful. Your job here is to uncover the ones that are creating your perfectionism, the intense pressure and loneliness of your life, and your denial of emotional pain.

Let's talk for a moment about trauma. If you were abused, traumatized, or neglected, you absorbed harsh and critical messages about what you should believe about yourself and about others. You might think, *I can never trust anyone... I deserved what I got... Nothing happened that was all that harmful... It was my fault.* How entrenched those beliefs are depends on many factors.

In abusive homes, the spoken and unspoken rules can be horrific and highly manipulative. They are meant to control. There's nothing rational about them. Perhaps you were labeled as "bad" by an angry parent and told, "Bad children don't get to eat." So you went hungry, even when you were trying to be "good."

Sometimes the rules are meant to cause confusion, and they change randomly and without warning. One day, you were allowed to use the computer. The next you weren't, but the switch was never stated. Your punishment was severe if these ever-changing rules weren't followed, keeping you confused and frightened.

And other rules are meant to conceal what is going on, whether abuse or neglect. No one spoke about Dad's drinking. And you somehow "knew" better than to ever talk about it. When there was no food in the fridge, but plenty of beer, you knew not to complain.

If you have suffered abuse, I recommend that you work with a therapist who can help you process your beliefs and the emotions that are locked in those memories of abuse. Please recognize that this book's specific focus isn't on healing sexual, physical, or emotional trauma. Rather, its focus is on perfectionism. But we cannot delude ourselves into thinking that the two have little to link them. Quite the opposite.

Unspoken rules can be found all over the place and can lead to a huge emotional reaction if they're challenged or broken. Mark's rules of what family "togetherness" looked like weren't tested until his eyes were opened by his wife's very different background.

*Mark's Story:* What "Togetherness" Is Supposed to Be

*When Mark was a child, every winter his entire family would go skiing. Aunts, grandparents, first and second cousins, siblings—anyone who was able to walk traveled to the annual mountain vacation. The rule was that everyone did everything together. All decisions were group decisions, such as where to eat lunch and what activities to do. People played games, sat by a roaring fire, shared the cooking and cleanup tasks. It had felt wonderful to Mark. He remembered tremendous closeness and camaraderie. And as an adult, he wanted his own children to experience the same.*

*Mark's wife, however, had grown up in a much more independent family. She chafed a bit at the "all for one and one for all" mentality and suggested one year that they take a couple of vacation days away to be together with their own children, privately. Mark rationally agreed that that was a great idea. But he fought a tremendous sense of disloyalty. He wondered if he wasn't appreciating the gifts his family offered or whether he was being selfish or not caring about his parents' feelings. An unspoken rule seemed to be: "You should always participate in everything."*

*The feelings of shame he had to fight—to simply spend some
alone time with his wife, son, and daughter—were intense.*

*The fallout from his family was indirect, for no one was
supposed to demonstrate disappointment either. He heard later
that his mom said something about his wife's family not being
"close." When their alone time ended and he, his wife, and
children returned to the fold, things were pleasant, but no
questions were asked about their days away. Mark was left with
emotions that were hard to pinpoint. He explained, "It was like
fighting a ghost. It wasn't tangible, but I knew the expectations
were there and very real." Yet, he also felt a strange sense of
welcome freedom.*

Both spoken and unspoken rules are vital to identify and understand. What were the rules in your childhood home?

### Reflection 35: Becoming Aware of Spoken and Unspoken Rules

This is an exercise that will require patience. Because as you recognize
each spoken or unspoken rule, there may be another hiding in the wings,
waiting for you to feel safe or strong enough to identify it. Take time to
write down the spoken and unspoken rules you learned from your family,
your culture, or your religion that most applied to you. You may want to
have each belief on its own page, because the next few reflections will be
built on them.

When you're done with the list, place parentheses around the rules
and beliefs that you no longer follow. Put a star by the ones that are still
highly active for you. As you write down these rules, what feelings emerge?
Whew… great work!

Step 2: Decide Whether Each Rule or Belief Serves You Well
in the Here and Now

This can be tricky because your thoughts could be so distorted
that they seem quite fine to you. In fact, you're so skilled in denying
pain that you can make anything seem healthy and constructive. So,

a good way to decide is to ask yourself, *Would I teach this belief to my daughter or son? Or to a good friend?* If the answer is a resounding *No!* then that's a huge clue that you shouldn't be applying it to your own life either. If you still wonder if your own distortions are getting in the way of assessing a rule's rationality, you can run the rule by a trusted friend to check out its appropriateness and ask for objective feedback.

Most self-destructive rules usually include absolutes: should, must, have to, always, never. These are black-and-white words that ignore the fact that healthy responses are often very situation specific. There might be instances when your rule is definitely the best way to go, and you can develop the skill of choosing when and where it should objectively be helpful. What's vital and very healing for you is that it's now your choice, rather than a mandate from the past. In the opening quote, Jon Kabat-Zinn points out that positively rigid thinking can be just as destructive as negatively rigid thinking. This is when you get to decide what's helpful in the here and now, and what's not.

Here's an old story to illustrate this point.

Gabrielle's husband, Jeff, watched her as she took a ham out of its packaging and cut a thick slice off the butt before she put it in to bake.

"Why do you do that?" he asked.

"You know, I don't know, but my mom always did it."

Gabrielle called her mom to find out. She asked, "Why do you cut off a slice of ham every time you bake one? Is that end not as tender?"

Her mom replied, "You know, I don't remember. I've just always done it like Noni."

Now both of them wanted to talk to Noni, the grandmother. And Noni erupted in roaring laughter when they asked her about it. She explained, "I cut it off because the only roasting pan I had back then was too small."

This is a funny story with a serious intent. Questioning the why, how, when, where, and what of things can certainly lend clarity to our actions and beliefs now. Recognizing that you may be blindly following rules that've been passed down or that you've simply unconsciously absorbed can be intensely freeing. And happily, there'll be more ham to go around.

### Reflection 36: What Beliefs Serve Me Well in the Here and Now?

Now you will begin to more carefully analyze your active rule system. Take the rules from the previous reflection and decide which rules fit the here and now. In what situations do the rules serve you well? In what situations do the rules not serve you well?

These recognitions may come to you quickly or they may require more time and energy before coming into your awareness. Keep at it... they will come.

### Step 3: Replace Old Destructive Rules with New Choices

I've observed that it usually takes risking a behavior change—making a different choice—before a belief can be totally challenged, decreased, or even eliminated. When you make a fresh choice based on your own belief in the present, you can free yourself from your own irrationalities. For example, if I allow myself to show my anger in my family and I do it appropriately, I'm likely to view that belief with fresh eyes—and realize I no longer want to be governed by that rule.

Think of all the movies that are based on characters challenging and breaking their former belief systems. *The Green Book*, 2018's Oscar-winning movie, was a fabulous example of how experiences that challenge an old belief system can greatly alter your perceptions of yourself and life. Change that is based on challenging the rationality of rules and the rigidity of your belief system can be extremely moving and powerful.

Your current beliefs—things that you're seeing as helpful and protective but actually aren't—can range from highly paralyzing (*I can never let anyone know the real me, I can never talk about what my stepfather did to me*) to those that aren't as serious but reflect how your past can govern your present. The greater the distortion, the more urgently you might've followed its regulations.

Let's take the belief *I can never let anyone know the real me.* In step 2, you asked yourself whether the belief you've held is constructive now. If it's not, then the next step is to risk creating a new rule (by telling yourself, for example, *I can choose to let someone into my inner world*) and deciding specifically where that new choice leads. For instance, you could say, *I'll tell one person that I'm reading this book.* Or, *I don't have to hide being overwhelmed. And I don't have to do everything that is asked of me at work.* What new choice might the new rule lead to now? You might decide, *Instead of automatically agreeing to an assignment at work and my anxiety going overboard, I'll be honest about my time frame and tell my boss I can get it done next week but not this one.*

Let's go over the process once more. Start with the rule (both spoken and unspoken). Decide whether it serves you well in the present. If it does, all good. If not, how do you want to change it and what specific behaviors will follow? Ask someone you trust if you doubt your own objectivity. Then it's time to take action. Start applying the new rule to your behavior.

Let's move to Juliette's story. It may seem frivolous, but I include it because I want you to understand that these irrationalities can exist on many levels. Hopefully, it will help you see some of the rules or beliefs you have absorbed without realizing it.

*Juliette's Story:* It Didn't Stop with Eyelashes

*When Juliette was a teenager, her mother convinced her that she looked sleepy if she didn't curl her eyelashes. She said, "Day after day, year after year, I curled the silly things, sometimes multiple times a day—until one morning, when my then-toddler was running all over the place, I threw the thing in the trash and decided I didn't care.*

*"Over the next few days I was certain that people were going to start offering me cups of coffee or ask if I'd slept. Neither happened. It was my mom who wanted my eyelashes*

*curled. It was her rule for women in general that they always
'look their best,' and she had her own version of that phrase.
I'd swallowed that version whole. It made me wonder at the
time, and even now, what other weird beliefs I might've
absorbed."*

*Juliette began to recognize the many rules governing her
behavior and which ones she could challenge and change.*

This process of reevaluation of your beliefs and rules can lead to
a sense of your life being rebooted and refreshed. Some rules and
beliefs are here to stay. You choose for them to continue to structure
your life and your behavior. Yet others can change. If anyone had
told me ten years ago that I'd believe I could write a book, I would've
laughed out loud. That was a definite new belief I had to develop.
What do you want yours to be?

**Reflection 37:** New Rules, New Choices, New Day

Now's the time to write out your new rules and the new choices that naturally follow. Create as many as you possibly can, again perhaps starting with
ones that would be easiest to implement, followed by those that might be
hardest. You could decide, "I don't want any more rules." But that's a bit
much. What new rules and beliefs about yourself or others do you want
to apply to your life now? They won't always be the opposite of the old
rule, or they might be. Set the bar as high as you're comfortable setting
it—knowing you can always come back and re-create.

Step 4: Experience the Feeling That Comes with Choosing
Your Own Rules

As you begin living by your new rules, what you were governed
by in the past—fear, guilt, shame, avoidance—will become clearer.
Remember the freedom that both Mark and Juliette felt? Initially,
they had to fight through a lot of unease and confusion. You'll get
there as well!

Also remember Laura's story. She felt guilt when she didn't do the automatic thing of taking on new responsibility. She got hit with feelings that she'd been avoiding by following her "I always volunteer" rule. She didn't know her place. She felt insecure. There was a part of her that wanted to fix it—to return to what she'd always said and done.

Familiar pain can be easier to feel than unfamiliar pain. You, like Mark, Juliette, and Laura, will be choosing the unfamiliar. And that takes guts.

It can be very powerful to experience letting go of a rule or belief that has held you hostage for many years, and then choose the unfamiliar path. And although very positive in many ways, it can feel extremely awkward and "wrong."

We'll talk in detail in Stage 4 about how to connect with those emotions and work through them.

# Connect with Emotional Pain for Healing

## *"It's Hard for Me to Feel"*

*"That's it, isn't it?" he answers, defeated.*

*"That's what?" I ask.*

*"You either feel it or live it, right? The pain. Either feel it or live it. Isn't that what you're going to say to me?"*

*"I wish there were easier options," I tell him. "I really do."*

—Terrance Real, author of *I Don't Want to Talk About It*

You've been busy challenging your belief systems and the rules that have governed your daily life. But now, you're likely to have become aware of something pretty uncomfortable: vulnerability. It can be terrifying to consider connecting with how you really feel—what's underneath your smiling persona. Looking in control, pleasing others, keeping your foot on the accelerator at all times—all these choices have protected you. Vulnerability's like shedding your armor when you're still in the middle of a battle. To confront shame head-on, to connect with your anger, to admit fatigue—it's too hard. It's too vulnerable. You can easily fear feeling far too exposed. And you can withdraw into whatever shell you can find. (Perhaps you remember the turtle analogy…)

You've read in many of the personal stories here that quiet aha moments can occur. New insight can shine a light on an old pattern that you now see as self-destructive. But that moment can easily be buried by what is a far more ingrained habit: emotional avoidance amid the distracting noise of everyday responsibilities. So, there's the battle. Do you let yourself obsess about getting one more task accomplished, or do you stop and wrestle with vulnerability? Do you approach and connect with your emotions, or do you withdraw?

I hope you choose vulnerability and connection. Because covering up, hiding, denying—all of the things that have kept you "safe"—have become dangerous.

So how do you connect with feelings that you've hidden from for so long?

Let me share another story. Back in the early nineties, I heard Maya Angelou speak at Bill Clinton's inauguration. I was blown away by the power of her presence. I'd just finished graduate school, so reading a book was not on my wish list. But I wanted to learn from her. At the bookstore, I found the shortest book she may ever have written, a collection of essays called *Wouldn't Take Nothing for My Journey Now* (1993). I was quite consumed at the time with my own need to appear put together, as I'd moved to Arkansas and was about to open my therapy practice.

One of those essays hit me in the gut. In it, she wrote about getting drunk in a local bar after being named "Person of the Week" by the *New York Post*. She felt very lonely even in the congratulatory crowd. Weaving slightly, she approached a table of men, sat down abruptly, and pummeled them with questions about why she was so unacceptable to their gender. "I sat and looked at each man for a long time, and then began a performance which now, more than twenty years later, can still cause me to seriously consider changing my name and my country of residence" (110).

Here was a poet laureate, a well-established celebrated author, admitting a very embarrassing moment in her life, painting herself as about as nonperfect as you could get. She was talking about shame—openly, honestly. And not in a tell-all dramatic way for attention but with candor and simplicity. I cried as I read, realizing more fully than ever the burden of shame and perfectionism I'd been carrying for far too long.

Maya Angelou allowed us to see her vulnerability. And that was incredibly powerful.

This chapter offers a similar lesson—that when you reveal not only your strengths but also your vulnerabilities, you can find peace and acceptance. You may feel discomfort along the way because you're no longer keeping yourself emotionally flat or covered up. And you can really feel again. Jealousy, resentment, anger, fear, sadness, shame, even your need to look perfect—you can admit and have compassion for their presence.

As the quote at the beginning of the chapter explains, you either feel it or live it. You either connect with pain or you mask it. The cost of not connecting with pain is that you live it out blindly, not being aware of how it's affecting you.

Tasha's story sheds light on how developing self-compassion and allowing feelings to emerge can change your life for the better.

### *Tasha's Story:* Perfect Obedience

*Tasha's mom was a severe alcoholic. Her parents divorced. But after a year or more of her mom going downhill, her father felt guilty about leaving the kids. He returned and remarried her mom. From then on, Tasha's dad made her very aware that he'd sacrificed his own happiness to save her. So, it became her job to show her gratitude by becoming who he wanted her to be. He was far from affectionate, but Tasha spent a lot of time trying to please him. The pressure was immense.*

*Although looking like the perfect child, she attempted suicide in high school. No one knew but her parents, who never asked her what had gone wrong—not when they picked her up at the hospital, not when she returned to school. Never.*

*As the family coped with the mother's continued drinking and highly jealous attitude toward her daughter, Tasha was molded by her dad. She became a partner in his small law firm. She said, "I never had any other dreams for myself. I didn't know what that was like."*

*Tasha married. Everyone told that her she had the perfect life: two children and a successful law practice, a husband who was faithful (although he was very similar to her dad, nonaffectionate and highly controlling).*

*While in therapy, Tasha finally found the feelings that she'd kept tightly sealed. She allowed herself to feel her anger toward both her parents. She cried over the emptiness of her marriage, seeing now how she'd re-created what was familiar to her. She didn't judge herself. She had compassion for the little girl who was obedient. She became aware of what emotions had been silently influencing her for years.*

*She divorced her husband, although fighting a tremendous fear of what others would think. Her children were surprised and devastated because, of course, Tasha had never looked unhappy. But they came to understand, as she blossomed into the mom and woman that could better express her feelings.*

Now let's learn a four-step process that will build structure for life-altering self-compassion to emerge as you create a road map of your experiences and memories.

## Building a Timeline to Achieve Emotional Awareness and Growth

Let's again ask: *How do I get to my feelings?* Your path has four steps:

1.  **Compassion:** viewing yourself through a warm, sensitive lens—the same lens you use with others.

2.  **Acknowledgment:** recognizing your feelings as normal and a natural consequence of the situation.

3.  **Mindful connection:** gently allowing emotions to emerge and connecting with them.

4.  **Acceptance:** accepting all you've discovered.

This process is more powerful than any armor. It may feel vulnerable at first but, in reality, that very vulnerability provides safety—because you're aware. You're present. There's no longer anything that can surprise or hurt you from the past. But it may feel like you're taking a tremendous risk. So let's create a structure that will help guide you. That structure is called a *timeline*. Creating a timeline of experiences can help you organize your life and your memories, and it can serve as a road map for your emotional experiences as well.

What is a timeline? It's a chronological ordering of powerful events and experiences you've had in your life that were important markers for you. In creating your timeline, you will write about experiences—both happy and painful—that were important to you in becoming who you are. Perhaps you met a mentor. A teacher was especially kind. You won a competition. You didn't get into the college you wanted, your beloved dog died, or a great friend moved away. Please consider all such impactful events.

Organize your timeline as you wish. One option is to draw a horizontal line and segment it into years. Then above the line you can write down positive experiences, below the line you can note traumatic or painful ones. You want to be able to view it easily so that you can see as much of it at one time as you can.

Creating a timeline will help you emotionally connect with pain from the past as well as begin to see how your present may be affected by your dismissal or denial of those events. So how do you get in a proper mind state to start this work? You follow your four-step path.

### Step 1. Compassion—Viewing Yourself Through an Empathic Lens

What exactly is *self-compassion?* It's extending kindness toward yourself. It's extending a generosity of spirit to you that differs greatly from self-pity, which defines you as a victim. Whatever happened to you in your life, however you coped with what was handed to you, whatever you've done that's healthy or not so healthy, self-compassion simply notices its impact, doesn't judge, and is present. And it's in that noticing that the next step—acknowledgment—can occur.

So, try to use self-compassion as you begin to create your time-line. You may have the urge to do this perfectly. Please resist that temptation. Be loving with yourself, as if you are guiding a child to do this work. You don't necessarily need to access the memories you've shoved into your emotion closet. In fact, it's preferable if you recall the ones that come easiest (we'll get to that closet later). Again, be kind to yourself; this work should not feel like torture.

You may remember a lot from your childhood or not. Some memories may be fuzzier than others. You may feel as if you don't have enough "big" memories. But if they were significant somehow, please include them. Nothing should be discounted. Remember, you're using a lens of compassion.

Here's a personal example of no memory being too small to include. I'll never forget my mother sitting down with me when I was around twenty-six. Looking concerned, she said, "I need to talk to you about something." I'd given her lots of reasons in the past to have "talks," but she'd never confronted me this seriously. Then she dropped the bomb: "Your weight is getting out of control." I'd recently married and gained about eight pounds, up to a whopping 120 (a weight that today I barely remember). The three-minute conversation was shaming to me and led to my anorexia recurring. Now I remember it as a signpost of my mother's own eating disorder and painful perfectionism. But that took me years to realize. And that's where being compassionate with yourself comes in. Instead of taking away shame from the experience, with self-compassion I could identify its impact more clearly.

**Reflection 38:** Creating My Timeline

For this exercise, you might want to use something in addition to your journal to create your timeline, as you might need more room. Allow yourself to go back and remember. What were the conversations, the events, the experiences that were important in shaping who you were? How did you learn that the world was safe or unsafe, kind or unkind, rational or irrational?

As you jot down the significant experiences that come to you, put them in chronological order. You don't have to stop with childhood. Continue into your adult years. Take your time. As you work, you may realize that you don't have many memories for a big chunk of your life or that one of your time frames may be chock-full of markers, some previously recognized and some not. Or you may tend to say to yourself, *That's not important enough.*

Once you have all the significant experiences written down, I invite you to dig deeper still. I'd like for you to add the memories you've compartmentalized—those you've stored in your emotion closet—if you haven't already done so. If you're struggling to remember, go back to Reflections 9 and 30. Your writing for those exercises can help you begin to fill out your timeline. Use as many pages as you need. You may likely need to journal as you go, as you validate both positive and negative experiences that were important.

You may want to do this over the course of several days or even weeks, as other experiences may emerge from your memory. You may or may not connect emotionally with the memories you discover. You may feel detached from what you've identified, or you may be caught off guard at how intensely you feel as you remember. If at any point this exercise brings up too-intense feelings, please seek professional support.

Shondra's story reveals how a timeline can help you organize and, perhaps for the first time, recognize the important experiences that shaped you into being you.

*Shondra's Story:* Going on Automatic

*Shondra grew up in a very supportive family. She'd been adopted and felt as loved and cherished as her siblings. When she was accepted to her dream college, she was ecstatic. But the loss of the security she'd always counted on was more than she anticipated. She felt uncomfortable. Everyone was an academic superstar. She told herself to get a grip. Her parents came to see her on Parents Weekend and told her she looked tired. "I'm fine—I'm really good," was her response.*

*When Marcus began paying attention to her, she fell hard. Very hard. He wanted to be with her every minute she wasn't in class. And she was right there for him. He hadn't had a great family, and she felt like he'd never been loved well. Her job became to fill that void.*

*When he began bossing her around and asking her to do things sexually she didn't want to do—while also beginning to call her vile names—she rationalized that this treatment came from the pain of his past. He'd ask forgiveness and she'd accept his apology. But the pattern became more and more demeaning, as he ramped up his demands. Over the three years they were together, her friends watched her change from being open and bright—a high achiever—to someone who was closed off—still smiling, still achieving, but on automatic pilot.*

*Shondra covered up her hurt and her pain. Only when she caught Marcus with someone else did she escape. But the damage had already been done. She decided then and there that no one would ever hurt her again. She'd stay in control for the rest of her life.*

*Shondra's solution was to wall herself off emotionally. Sex with her husband became another duty to be ticked off the list, far from a more vulnerable, true intimacy, and they fought about their intimate relationship on a regular basis. It was only when she had everything in her life that could bring her happiness that she realized something was terribly wrong. She was horribly lonely.*

*She'd always blamed her discomfort with being vulnerable sexually on the fatigue of rearing children and a strenuous work schedule, never realizing its connection with how Marcus had hurt her. Yet when she built her timeline, she could see that Marcus's sexually abusive treatment of her was a turning point in her life. Her absorption of shame had caused her to withdraw, to distrust others, and to have difficulty with opening up in relationships. Shondra confided in her husband, and they began a completely different conversation about intimacy than had been possible before.*

So, again, take the time you need. You're not accustomed to thinking of your life with compassion, with going back in time and very gently remembering what you felt like in that present moment. But those experiences led you to begin to hide and develop the survival strategies you did. If you're struggling to remember or have fragments of memory, consider reaching out to your best friend at the time, a family member, an ex-boyfriend or -girlfriend, or a teacher who knew you back then. They may have information that would be very helpful for you to be able to put more of the pieces of the puzzle in place. Of course, that means letting them in on your journey. But reaching out, in and of itself, could propel you forward in this very worthwhile effort to identify the experiences that shaped you into who you are now.

### Step 2: Acknowledgment—Recognizing the Messages You Learned

There's something important to discuss before we head forward, and that's the difference between *blame* and *acknowledgment*. There are plenty of people who believe that therapy involves blaming your parents or your past for who you are now. There could be nothing farther from reality. In fact, anyone stuck in blame will only become bitter. That's not helpful at all.

This step isn't about blame, it's about acknowledgment. Acknowledgment is recognition. It's owning that something existed or exists. Your search for healing is all about acknowledgment and the power it brings. Please try to catch yourself if you get lost in the idea that you're blaming. I promise you—if you follow these steps, you're not.

We absorb messages about ourselves from the experiences we have. This step involves acknowledging what those messages were. The experiences on your timeline carried a message to you, whether intentional or unintentional, positive or painful. For example, if the event is that your best friend died in a car accident, the (unintentional) message you'd learn might be, "People I care about can suddenly disappear from my life," or "If I love, I can get hurt."

Often the most damaging messages are ones that teach us whether we are loved or valued, whether we feel safe or protected. These memories often involve neglect, loss, abuse, or bad parenting. So, it's very helpful to pinpoint the messages from those timeline experiences. These are often the aha moments that I've talked about before, moments when you make a connection between a past event and the message it held (and may still hold) for you. Think about some of the stories you've read thus far. Tasha learned, "My value is in becoming who my father needs me to be," while Tony believed, "As long as I'm a star, I'll be loved."

Let's break this down further. Ask yourself two questions about each timeline memory as you acknowledge its message to you.

1. *What message did I get from this experience about myself or about life?*

2. *What did I absorb and come to believe about my capability of being loved, safe, and valued from this experience?*

Let's take my conversation with my mom about my weight as an example.

1. *What message did I get from this experience about myself or about life?*

The message I got was that I wasn't acceptable to her if I wasn't thin.

2. *What did I absorb and come to believe about my capability of being loved, safe, and valued from this experience?*

If I morph myself into what others need me to be, then I'll be loved.

There's no right or wrong in what you decide the messages were. The messages will be unique to you—but also are part of our shared human experience. We all have absorbed messages like these, whether intentionally sent or not. If you struggle, talk to your buddy about it, ask a trusted friend, or consider sessions with a therapist.

You can hear the power of these messages. They led you to the survival strategies you developed to hide the pain. You want to acknowledge that power. Why? Because these messages can shape your life for the good, or they can lead you in directions that are self-destructive and harmful, such as perfectly hidden depression.

After the brief discussion with my mom, I allowed the power of her message to reactivate my previous anorexic behavior. Then I hid more from my parents about the next few years of my life, feeling that I couldn't let them truly know what my struggles were. Notice I wrote "allowed." It's important to take responsibility for my own part while acknowledging that the message was significant and very real to me. You'll want to do a similar thing. Look for how much you allowed the message to stick or be absorbed.

You may still be holding on to the idea that this is all about blaming, as we discussed previously. If so, try using the reasoning I offered before. Ask yourself, *If my best friend told me about these experiences in his life, would I understand how he might have felt?* Yes! You're making the huge step of not discounting or denying but acknowledging. You're looking through a compassionate lens and acknowledging the normalcy of what you absorbed: *Oh, of course, I felt that way. Anyone would've felt that way if they'd received this message.* If, for some reason, you now realize that the message you absorbed was somehow faulty or mistaken, that can be healing as well.

**Reflection 39:** Putting Together the Memories
and the Messages

Now it's time, if you haven't begun already, to return to your timeline and acknowledge what you've learned from each significant marker. Ask yourself the two questions for each memory on your timeline: *What message did I get from this experience about myself or about life?* And *What did I absorb and come to believe about my capability of being loved, safe, and valued from this experience?*

Again, this may take a fair amount of time, given whatever number of events or experiences you've identified. Keep your answers in your now well-used journal, so that you can read them over.

You may have to do some digging to get to what you learned. Your perfectly hidden depression may rear its head and say, "Now, now, it wasn't that bad. Or that serious. Or that awful." But you've gotten this far! You can confront that voice. The discovery of what you walked away believing—what has led you to be self-critical and shaming—is another step in the recognition of what was, and may still be, unhealthy and self-destructive. Please journal about these realizations—you're taking huge steps forward in putting together the memories with the messages. Good job!

Step 3: Mindful Connection—Being Present with
Your Emotions

In this step, as you fully acknowledge the messages you received, you want to allow your emotions to come to the surface. You want to feel the absorbed message's emotional impact. If the message was from a more positive experience, such as winning an award or having someone in your family go out of their way to make time for you after school, those messages might have been: "When I try hard, I can accomplish a lot." Or, "I felt loved simply because I existed." Emotions created from these messages could be pride and feeling secure. These positive emotions may be easier for you to allow than painful ones. Yet sometimes, when you've become expert at compartmentalization, all intense feelings get stored away, whether they're happy or not. Allowing yourself to feel any emotion deeply may be hard for you.

Particularly if the message was harmful or demeaning, it can be more difficult for you to connect with its resulting emotion. You've been avoiding the pain for a long time. You may say to yourself, *But I don't like feeling sad or angry or afraid. It feels wrong somehow.* And yet there's no emotion that makes you "bad." In fact, if you allow your emotion to surface and are mindful of its presence, you're much more likely to recognize when it's affecting you.

Remember the quote at the start of this chapter: "Either feel it or live it." Maybe you feel uncomfortable connecting with anger. Maybe you resist the tears that come to your eyes. Yet when you avoid feeling, that emotion can boomerang and affect you in ways you can't necessarily identify. You're beginning to anchor emotions to a memory and a message. Allowing your emotions to surface is key to being present.

What do I mean by being "present"? Being present with an emotion is allowing it to run its course without trying to avoid it, deny it, or run away from it. This is when your practice of mindfulness plays a vital role in your healing process. You have to be still and clear your mind from thoughts that might want to distract you, visualize yourself at the time of the event or experience, and feel what comes. It may be slow at first. That's okay. Simply allow what's there to surface.

Imagine standing in a rain shower on a warm, spring day. If you allow yourself, you can immerse yourself in the experience. You can smell the smells, feel the water on your skin, and hear the rain's own quiet rhythm. Maybe you've done something similar at a music concert, a movie, a theater performance, or while reading a book. You've gotten lost in the music or the plot. It's all very real to you right then and there. You're in the experience, not looking at it or watching yourself be there. That's being present. That's being mindful. And that's what you want to create now.

Yet if the emotions are painfully strong, being present with them can feel as if you could be crushed by them. If this is the case, or you fear that it might be, four things could be very helpful:

- You can actively visualize a place where you feel secure and go there in your mind if needed.

- You can use your meditative practice to not fuel the pain but to simply note it and let it go.

- You can find safety through writing. Instead of allowing the emotion to gather steam and take you somewhere that's destructive, writing can give it shape and form, or a beginning and an end.

- You could ask someone to be with you and to be there for you.

That said, take breaks from this process. Do something you haven't done in a long time that you've missed. Go on a walk or get moving in a way that feels good. Make sure you have movies you could watch or music that you could listen to that can ease the tension. That's the kind of distraction that can be healthy and constructive.

I cannot stress enough that although this work may be something you're able to do, it may not be safe for you to do it alone. If there's trauma, abuse, or neglect in your history, finding a therapist that has experience with these dynamics is not just advisable but may be necessary. Please give yourself permission to do so. You can find safety in a supportive therapeutic relationship that you can't necessarily feel in any other.

### Reflection 40: What Emotions Were Brought Up by My Timeline?

If you haven't begun already, return to each marker on your timeline and acknowledge its message. Again, don't simply write about your feelings—risk feeling them as you write. Remember the earlier research quoted. You don't want to *describe* the emotion, you need to *express* it. Skip an emotion if it doesn't emerge at first. Go on to the next and return to that one when you can.

Journal about what and how you're feeling, seeing your life through your timeline and the messages you received. What surprises you? What doesn't? How does it cause you to feel overall? How does it lead you to self-compassion, if indeed it does? What do you understand and see now that wasn't as clear to you before creating your timeline?

### What If I Still Don't Feel Anything?

You're highly skilled in intellectualizing, in staying in your head instead of connecting with your heart. Many times, I've watched someone on the verge of letting go, of allowing an emotion to surface—only to quickly blink it away or awkwardly change the subject.

If this is you, you may be asking yourself, *So, how do I reach my feelings?* You can revisit Reflection 3 as a start. Explore what you're scared to feel. What have you told yourself is wrong to feel? It could be confusion. Fear. Disappointment. Joy. Anger. Sadness. Contentment. Shame.

If you immediately feel discomfort at even the thought of expressing the emotion, then stay in the moment—stay with that discomfort. Be mindful of it. It's a huge clue. See what your mind and heart bring to the table. See if it's tied to a message that you've identified from your timeline. Give it time and space.

Your unease or discomfort with your emotions reveals what you learned and what you still mistakenly believe now. This is incredibly important for your own emotional growth.

If you're struggling, pull up one memory on your timeline when you can identify the message but you can't connect with the feeling. Now go back in time. Describe the situation in detail. For example, "It was right after my parents separated. All I remember is that Mom started acting weird, dressing way too young, and going out with her friends, while Dad seemed preoccupied and really sad. No one paid much attention to me. The message was, 'You don't have enough value for us to care about you.' I remember how they felt, but what did I feel?" As you take yourself back to that time and place, you can identify more specifically how you felt. You're accustomed to tuning out your own emotions and tuning in to others' feelings. It will take some practice to pay attention and connect with your own.

Three things may be getting in your way. First, you may not want to look weak. Many people associate showing emotion with weakness or being out of control. Take crying, for example. I've said before that tears represent intensity. Whether you cry out of joy, sadness, or anger, your tears reflect the depth of your feeling. Changing this very stoic belief can help you risk showing some kind of vulnerability. You're taking down that wall of yours slowly but surely.

Second, you may have convinced yourself that your feelings get in the way of making good decisions. Your immediate feelings shouldn't govern your choices. But there's a concept called *emotional intelligence,* which stresses what our emotions can do for us to ensure a fulfilling and productive life. Your curiosity, being able to distinguish between wants and needs, empathy, passion—all are aspects of emotional intelligence. Far from being a detriment to good decision making, your emotional intelligence is extremely vital in making good choices.

Third, you may be very tuned out of the messages your body is sending you. Your body often gives you clues that emotions are occurring. Your heart may race. Your stomach may tighten. Or the opposite—you may feel tension glide off of you or your breathing may become calm. This kind of dissociation from your body can make it very difficult to identify what your body is telling you or to determine where you feel certain emotions. If you're using substances like alcohol or weed to mute your feelings, they may remain totally out of your reach.

### Reflection 41: Reconnecting with Safer Emotions

If you're still having trouble with more-intense emotions, find one that's easier to feel. Let's say you felt disappointed when your basketball team lost the state championship and you easily remember how that felt. Practice asking yourself questions about it: *Where do I feel it in my body? What color or shape could it be?* Sit and be with how it feels to be disappointed. If you can allow yourself to remember fully how it felt, that's practice for doing the same with more-intense emotions that are harder for you. You can use every sense you have to deeply connect with it. Then you can return to the more-intense emotion and follow the same process.

If you can't connect with any of your emotions after you've tried to do these things, you may need to consider that you've become clinically depressed, a symptom of which can be a flat or blunted emotional presentation. Check back into Chapter 2 to help you make that determination, and reach out to a therapist or physician to further discuss.

### Other Helpful Activities

Here are a few additional things you can do to help with this emotional work:

- **Consult a word list of emotions.** You may benefit from a list of emotions to help you identify what, exactly, you're feeling. You're so accustomed to not feeling that you may not have names for them. This happens more than you might realize. Websites like TherapistAid.com offer free downloads of such a list.

- **Join a therapy group.** Or form a support group of your own. This can be immensely helpful, as there's nothing like meeting with people who are dedicated to being honest, open, and curious about what will help them move forward. They'll have your back, and they may also point out things to you that you may be missing. National groups such as Adult Children of Alcoholics, as well as local therapists and churches, may be running groups for abuse and/or neglect, grief, divorce, or self-development.

- **Reach out to that now-trusted friend.** Tell them about one or more of your memories. When you see the compassion in their eyes, it may very well allow you to release your own emotions.

- **Watch movies that pull for emotion.** There are a ton of them—everything from *Dead Poets Society* to *The Impossible* to *The Color Purple* to *Room*.

- **Listen to music that pulls for emotion.** Samuel Barber's "Adagio for Strings" always leads me to my sadness and grief. Country music songs are good for that as well. Try Miranda Lambert's "The House That Built Me" or Trace Adkins's "You're Gonna Miss This."

- **Seek out calming touch and physical release.** Bessel van der Kolk in *The Body Keeps the Score* (2014) reminds us of the importance of touch to help soothe our emotions, which can even lead to feeling them more deeply. "Touch, the most elementary tool we have to calm down, is prescribed from most therapeutic practices. Yet you can't fully recover if you don't feel safe in your skin. Therefore, I encourage all my patients to engage in some sort of bodywork, be it therapeutic massage, Feldenkrais, or cranio-sacral therapy" (218). Whatever you like, your body can and will respond. It's another avenue for healing.

- **Do something active to get in touch with anger.** Crashing old glass mason jars against a wall, buying a stuffed animal that represents someone in your life and beating it up, taking kickboxing lessons—all these things can help you find and express your anger in a tangible, real way. Look for something that fits you. You may have a little cleanup to do, but it can be incredibly cathartic.

Step 4: Awareness—Realizing Unconscious Patterns
and Relationships

This step is exciting as you grow in your awareness of and insight into patterns that have come into your consciousness. You begin by wondering how the events or experiences of your timeline influenced you. You can begin to question, *If X hadn't happened, would Y have happened?* Or, *Could Y be happening now because X happened in the past?* You saw this very powerfully in Shondra's story.

Step back a little from your timeline and see how you were shaped by these experiences and the messages and emotions linked to them. How is each related to the others? Does one seem to lead to another? Is there a theme or repetitive pattern in your thinking or behavior that you can recognize? Can you make the connection that a feeling you have in the present is similar to a feeling you had before? Let yourself begin to wonder and see where your mind and heart take you.

Jeffrey saw his pattern clearly. "I always got the message from my mother that I was the responsible one—so I took care of the younger kids. I was fixing dinner for them when I was six and getting them up for school when I was nine… I just assumed, when I married, that I'd be financially responsible for our family, and I never expected my spouse to work. Now I'm growing resentful."

Some themes will stand out boldly, and it may be easy to identify the pattern of how one event mirrors another, how the present mimics the past, and how similar your emotional reactions are to each experience. You might be able to make the connection, *If this hadn't happened, perhaps this wouldn't have either.* Or vice versa: *Since this happened, it set me up to see things this way and make this choice.*

**Reflection 42:** Beginning to Recognize Themes
and Patterns

Please write out these initial themes and patterns of behavior. A theme might be "fear of rejection" or "shame for feeling sadness." The themes are innately connected to the message you received earlier, whether as a child or an adult.

Look over your timeline to see just how many events are tied together thematically. This might be another opportunity when you share your timeline with your buddy and get their perspective on what themes they can identify in your life. Two heads are better than one, right?

Consider this analogy: You're standing very close to a mirror. Very close. You can't see very well, can you? But if you step back, your total vision improves. You can see more of the whole, rather than a small piece. That's what you're doing with your timeline. That's what you're doing with your buddy. That's the gift you're giving yourself—to create a broader view of what made you…you.

Hopefully, Mallory's story will help you see what these steps can do for you.

*Mallory's Story:* Making Emotional Connections

*Mallory's childhood had been highly chaotic, with a mom who in one minute was frenetically involved with her kids and in the next was abusively critical and harsh. Her father tried to mop up whatever mess his wife left. Mallory had fragments of memories of sexual abuse by neighborhood boys that disturbed her. Yet she also had a vague sense that her mom had known but did nothing. She felt blamed for seeing the problems others denied, and she had always felt she was the black sheep among the children. Now, as an adult, Mallory helped take care of her mom and dad, had good relationships with her siblings, and had created a successful life.*

*She only came into therapy because she was suffering from stomach and gut problems that had worsened substantially when she exercised, something she'd done obsessively as a distraction from feeling anything about her childhood. As Mallory created her timeline, she could see and begin to express the pain of her childhood. It was hard for her. She was one tough cookie.*

*She began working through the confusion and pain of being
sexually abused—and of not being believed. She felt anger
toward her dad, as well as tenderness. She had both contempt
and empathy for her mom. She recognized the messages that
were inherent in her parents' treatment of her and her siblings.
The critical label she'd always applied to herself as the black
sheep was confronted. She could recognize there wasn't any
evidence that she'd been a hard child to love or parent. She
stopped taking responsibility for her parents' difficulties.
She hated to cry, but occasionally a tear would appear for
an instant or two. She began believing in her own worth.*

*As Mallory studied how her timeline had affected her, in
both good and painful ways, she began looking in the present.
She suddenly realized how her own patterns of mothering were
inconsistent. She explained, "You know, when my children need
me or want to tell me something, I feel like I'm a good mom.
But I quickly become overwhelmed with them wanting to sit by
me or hold on to me. I have to fight the urge to get up and go to
my bedroom. I win that battle most of the time, but I've never
figured out why—until now. Now I can see that what I got from
my own mom was so all over the place. I don't know how to be
comfortable with being emotionally wanted or available."*

*It's also highly intriguing to note that as Mallory connected
with her past and her emotions, her stomach issues receded, and
her exercise became something she once more relished.*

This is your work now. It's important to see in Mallory's story
that it wasn't only the analysis of her timeline that helped her
become who she is now; she also had to feel and have compassion for
the child she was. As you analyze your own markers, as you identify
the strong messages you received, as you feel what you must have felt
as a child or as an adult, as you allow those feelings to surface and
they reveal what you came to believe, then you can look around and
see how those patterns may be repeating themselves in your life now
and in your relationships with others. This is where you can begin

true insight and notice when those old messages are popping into your head. That insight can lead to true change.

The next and final stage of healing may seem self-explanatory. It's called Change. But we'll also be discussing the freedom you can begin to experience with risk and exploration, and the different kinds of energy it takes to initiate versus maintain change. I'll suggest specific risks to begin taking, or you can certainly devise your own.

You're doing a spectacular job by making it this far! You may want to take some time to go back through Stages 3 and 4, writing in your journal as is helpful. Take your time. You're getting close to becoming perfectly imperfect.

# Change Your Focus from Perfection to True Happiness

## *"I Want to Risk Self-Acceptance. Where Will My Journey Lead?"*

*A Native American wisdom story tells of an old Cherokee who is teaching his young grandson about life. "It is a terrible fight and it is between two wolves. One is evil—he is anger, envy, sorrow, regret, greed, arrogance, self-pity, guilt, resentment, inferiority, lies, false pride, superiority, and ego. The other is good—he is joy, peace, love, hope, serenity, humility, kindness, benevolence, empathy, generosity, truth, compassion, and faith. The same fight is going on inside of you—and inside every other person too." The grandson thought about it for a minute and then asked his grandfather, "Which wolf will win?" The old Cherokee simply replied, "The one you feed."*

—Kristin Neff, author of *Self-Compassion*

The wisdom of the Cherokee teaching used to introduce this chapter is simple: the part of you that you feed is the part of you that will flourish. What does it mean to feed some part of you? It's your focus—where you live and spend your time in your mind and heart. You've lived in self-criticism. You've lived in fear of making a mistake or faltering in any way. You've lived under constant pressure. Yet, with every page turn of this book, every reflection written, and every emotional connection made, you've begun feeding the good wolf inside of you.

## What You Will Find When You Risk Change

In the introduction, I planted a seed that with each risk attempted, you would gain hope in lasting change. That hope becomes the fuel for more risk and more change, thus setting up your own healing cycle.

Now, in this stage called Change, the focus is on taking more of those risks. I've already asked you to do certain things that involved becoming more open, such as sharing your timeline with a buddy or telling one person that you trust about reading this book.

Yet you still may be waiting in the wings, not sure whether you're comfortable with or ready to make any changes that would be life altering. As you've read and written, you may have realized how restricted your life has been, governed by rules that weren't healthy when you began to follow them and certainly aren't now. You may recognize that the emotions you've allowed yourself to show have been carefully selected for their appropriateness and that the more powerful emotions, the ones that might've revealed more of your identity or your struggle, have been locked up tightly. But to totally risk a new way of being? One that doesn't look as neat or well put together?

That's a daunting task. First, you have to conquer your fear.

## How to Conquer Your Fear

It's hard to trust that these changes will help. Perfectionism is the way you've survived. If you'd been thrown out of a boat into the ocean and I called out for you to unbuckle the life preserver you were wearing so that you'd be free to put on a stronger, better one that was coming your way, but just out of sight, would you do it? You'd look at me like I was crazy. How in the world are you supposed to trust that something better is coming? How are you supposed to cope with the terror that will grip you as soon as you are battling the waves alone?

It's very hard to believe, at least at first, that throwing out ingrained survival strategies and replacing them with new ones will actually lead to a greater sense of security and well-being. There's a specific battle going on inside of you between two voices. The evil wolf's voice demands more perfection and more covering up, while the good wolf's voice has been quietly building strength through the years. It's fighting for a fuller, freer life. It's saying, "Risk leaning into your fear of vulnerability."

That second wolf knows you could drown under the barrage of inflexible demands made by the evil wolf. And it's warning you that you could lose the battle, even though the good voice is fighting hard.

Please listen to this warning. Admit your fear. Sit with it and address each fear one at a time, while emotions previously suppressed are headed your way. You might notice I didn't say, "Get rid of your fear." No, let it be. Sit with it. Feel it and, as you can, gently release what you can. When you don't run away from or avoid fear, it loses its power to control you.

Remember the much earlier reference to the game of Jenga?

Think about the game. You carefully pull one piece out, and all is well. You pull another piece out and perhaps one falls, but things are still fairly stable. Each pull is a risk, and much of the game can fall down around you. Once you begin openly risking change, making connections, realizing the emotional impact of one event or experience in your life, then your life may feel as if it's falling apart. Strong new emotions may swoop into your consciousness.

There's no way to do away with the risk or the ambiguity of not knowing what's next. To take that risk—to trust that second voice and allow yourself to experience your vulnerability—is life changing.

### How to Sit with Vulnerability

Letting go of perfectionism takes an acceptance of risk and the vulnerability that comes with it. You aren't perfect. You don't have to look perfect or act perfectly. Your weaknesses are going to show to others. (Theirs do to you, right?)

Sitting with your vulnerability means that you can admit that both the good and the evil wolf exist in you and that the best you can do is try to feed the one that's fighting for love and compassion. There will be times when you feel jealous, when you wallow in self-pity, or when you're insensitive or overreactive. Those are emotions and actions we all fall into. They are what make all of us imperfect. Admitting them, living with them, others knowing them because you told them—all of it takes vulnerability.

I'll use my experience as a new author as an example of sitting with vulnerability. I became paralyzed about halfway through the writing process and spent several days staring at a blank screen. What was causing so much fear? As I grappled with my own feelings, I wrote the following paragraph to you, my potential reader, early one morning, not sure how or even if I'd use it.

"One of the daunting tasks of writing this book is the almost constant realization that there is much wisdom out there about the process of change and growth—with only the tiniest bit known by me. In many ways, I wish I had a lifetime to write, as the fear exists that the minute I finish, I'll learn something new, remember something I forgot to say, read an exceedingly enlightening quote I've never seen, or watch a patient discover something that might be helpful to you in your own journey. But that's my own perfectionism talking to me and my discomfort with vulnerability. Can you hear it? I bet you can. So, I have to find my own peace that this book will be an imperfect guide for you to grow more comfortable with your own imperfection. It seems a bit ironic, but I have to sit in my own vulnerability. And live there. Unapologetically. For good."

After I wrote this, I wasn't stuck anymore. Acceptance of your own vulnerability makes it much easier to take risks. Because if you fail or struggle, that failure or struggle doesn't define you any more than your success would. You learn from those failures. You don't have to hide them.

Acceptance of vulnerability brings with it freedom.

### The Slow, Steady Journey Through Grief to Freedom

In your own battle with perfectly hidden depression, self-acceptance can bring freedom from being imprisoned by old rules. Freedom from the tension of living very cautiously and vigilantly, carefully monitoring your life so you don't lose control. Freedom to openly express your true emotions in the moment. Freedom to create true intimacy with the ones you love.

Even freedom to finish a book.

This journey requires a slow, steady energy and persistence. What do I mean by that?

When you first begin to change habits and behaviors, the results can be heady. Think about starting a new job or having a new baby. You may be on a high with energy galore, simply because of the rush of how new it all feels. But then comes reality. You find out your commute is longer than you thought, or the supervisor who hired you left the company. The baby may be colicky, or your two-year-old may be sulking that she now has to share the attention. Things can go from high to hard pretty quickly.

As we discussed before, in your own growth, things might even feel worse before they feel better. As you've let off the brakes and allowed feelings in, they can arrive with such force that you'll have to steady yourself or reach out for help. Think about how long you've been covering up—feeling angry and suppressing it, feeling sad and getting even busier, or not feeling at all, ever.

You may even question why in the world you picked up this book, wondering what it would be like to forget all of this and go back to your perfect-looking persona. Lonely but perfect looking. Depressed but perfect looking. You can be overwhelmed by feelings that you've never had to handle before. The first few times you do, you may feel even darker than ever.

One of those feelings that can "feel worse" may be a deep grief. Grief that you were hidden for so long. Grief about opportunities not taken because of your perfectly hidden depression. Grief about the circumstances or the trauma that led to the creation of your perfectly hidden depression. This is a normal part of any healing process. As you recognize and gain new information about what it's like to live your life differently, you can get angry or sad that you were needlessly hidden for so long. You may have to mourn both what was and what was not.

That's when your own self-compassion plays a role. It wasn't needless at the time. It served its own purpose.

I wish I had a nickel for every time someone has looked at me with anger or despair, sadness or sarcasm, and said, "So why is it that I couldn't have figured this out before? Why couldn't I know then what I know now?"

Because you can't. That's why. Because it takes living life one day at a time to gain the experience, wisdom, and courage needed to recognize and heal your own vulnerabilities. Again, your goal is self-acceptance. And that self-acceptance includes what you may now wish you'd known earlier.

### Reflection 43: Allowing My Grief to Emerge

Please take the time to allow yourself to connect with the grief you feel over spending so much of your life trapped by your perfect-looking persona. Journal about what perfectly hidden depression may have cost you emotionally, physically, spiritually, and relationally, and what it feels like to fully realize that in this moment.

At some point, perhaps at many points in this process, stop and reread what you've written and allow your grief to bubble up and be as real to you as the air you breathe. You no longer have to fear feeling it. Stay in this place as long as you need. Your grief may emerge during different parts of this process, not only in this exercise. It could be anger or sadness. When it comes, breathe through it and with it. This very hard-earned moment—grieving what has been—will also help you let go and move in new directions.

Spencer met with substantial grief after she risked sharing her most important secret.

### Spencer's Story: Discovering Grief

*Spencer went to therapy to learn how to approach her parents with a secret that she'd kept for years—that she was gay. She desperately feared rejection. Although she'd been living with her partner, Claire, for well over three years, she had her own, separate home; when family would visit, she'd welcome them there with open arms.*

*A cheerful, smart, hardworking woman in her late twenties, Spencer talked at her law firm about things she and Claire did over the weekends. But she was afraid of rejection there as well. She was popular and funny, keeping everyone in stitches. But when not headed to Claire's, her nights were far from funny. They would be spent sitting in the dark, worrying and overeating.*

*Her parents had been loving but had given her the message over the years that they didn't think she was quite smart enough to be successful, and she'd been determined to prove them wrong. They also were conservatively religious, and although they'd never mentioned any problems with being gay, the subject wasn't discussed. They often told her that they worried because she was alone. They asked her about dating; her answers remained vague.*

*Her mom shared way too much about her own problems, and Spencer dutifully listened and gave advice for hours. So much of her own life was sequestered, she didn't have much to talk about except work, so focusing on her mom was easy. Claire, whose family knew and supported the couple, was growing impatient.*

*The day finally came when Spencer felt ready, and she mailed a letter to her folks. A few days later, her parents called. She was shocked to discover that they were very supportive. They both said, "It's good to know that you're not alone." They talked extensively the following weekend and asked to meet Claire. When that happened a few weeks later, things couldn't have been better. And Spencer and Claire began to plan to get married.*

*That's when Spencer's grief became palpable. Why had she spent so much time and effort hiding? She ruminated about time missed and opportunities lost. She was angry as she lashed out, "I've wasted a whole decade of my life trying to be what I thought others expected." Before any planning could continue, her work was to sit with that grief and all of its components.*

Spencer's story is about a literal secret that kept her real life and emotions locked away. You may have had similar secrets and ones that you believed if anyone "knew" they'd reject you. But the true import of her story is that grief can await you when you realize time lost or opportunities missed. Your tendency to shame yourself can pick up steam here and try to infiltrate your thinking. Please don't allow that. Instead, realize you couldn't have known what would've happened *if…* there are far too many unknown possibilities. You only know for certain what happened. If there's grief, write about it, talk about it, and feel it.

### Reflection 44: Honoring the Years of Wearing the Mask

It's important to honor the years that you wore a mask. What can be healing is to write about what you learned during this period of time. What is the meaning now of those years? Look at yourself compassionately. What did you need to learn or experience? Why is now the time when you've chosen to unveil yourself?

It's also important to consider how this life-altering work might not have been possible before. Maybe your support system is better, your kids are older, or you've gotten through a rough few years. Perhaps you've gained in maturity. Continue from Reflection 43, Allowing My Grief to Emerge, and work through the emotions that these questions bring.

Hopefully, you've gained a lot of insight in the prior stages. Maybe you've even risked voicing more of your feelings or saying no to a request. Congratulations if that's the case! But if not, that's okay as well. Everyone's journey will be different. Yet hope doesn't emerge solely from insight. That's why risking is so important. Hope comes when you see your actual choices and behavior change in the present, when you can put your head on your pillow at night and realize, *I did something today that I never thought I could do.* Your grief, however palpable, can begin to be healed—because you can see yourself changing. You have proof that you can stop covering up, and each new risk leads to more freedom.

## Getting Down to the Brass Tacks of Change

We've talked about facing your fear, sitting with vulnerability, and trudging through grief to freedom. Now it's time to allow the power of that awareness to spur you into action—if you haven't already done so. Remember, insight is wonderful and very helpful. But where you get hope is from new action and from behavior change. It's time for that action.

Let's revisit the ten directions we outlined in Stage 3. We'll use them as guideposts. And then I'll ask you to identify three situations in your life where you can name the specific risk that you feel ready to take. I'll give examples, but these risks will be unique to you. Write each new risk in your journal, listing them so that you can define them clearly.

## Moving Toward Loosening the Grip of Perfectionism

There are two components that must be dealt with when moving in this direction: perfectionism itself and the shaming voice that drives it forward.

### Perfectionism Itself

What do you as a perfectionist fear the most? Being seen as incompetent, caught not looking put together, or worse, disappointing to those who you believe expect perfection from you. If something is not perfect, that equates with failure. Now, this may not apply to everything in your life. You may be able to go to the grocery store without makeup. You may be able to talk to your boss about certain problems. But for the things that matter to you, really matter, your yardstick changes. That critical voice inside stands ready to judge harshly and plunge you into shame.

## Reflection 45: Challenging the Label of "Incompetence"

Write three specific actions in your journal that you fear would earn you the label of "out of control." (Remember, the risk is your own perception.) Then identify the risk, such as "In my next committee meeting I'll end it by asking for suggestions on how to proceed—and risk looking like I'm not sure of the best direction." Or, "During my reunion weekend with friends, I'll be honest and confide that my teenager is messing around with drugs—and risk looking like a bad parent." Or, "When Stacy comes over this afternoon, I'll leave the unfolded laundry out on the table—and risk looking disorganized."

All of these examples reflect you freeing yourself from your own perceptions of perfection.

Now decide which one of your three actions would be the easiest for you to risk. Then screw up your courage and do it. This is when you begin to choose how to live your life instead of being governed by fear. Those around you may be a little surprised. But remember, you're doing this for yourself, not for them.

### Your Shaming Voice

Years ago, a supervisor said to me, "Shame is a helpful emotion—if it lasts for ten seconds and leads to a change in behavior." After years of being a therapist, I couldn't agree more. The problem emerges when shame is near constant and overly critical.

So, let's start changing the behavior of self-shame. Begin by doing small things that your critical voice would tell you aren't "important" or "productive enough" or "not part of the plan for the day." You want to honor whatever mood or feeling you have right at that moment. Drive straight past the dry cleaners (where you need to pick up clothes) and go get some ice cream. Get up and do something on Saturday morning that's completely spontaneous. Take a mental health day off from work and don't fill it with tasks but go do something nice for yourself. Okay… start with a mental health afternoon if you can't swing the whole day.

Your inner critic is what has prevented you from being in the present because you think you have to keep things going in the "right" direction. Just get in your car and literally drive in whatever direction you want to in the moment. Go see what you can see. And if you drive into a rainstorm, laugh and decide that a rainstorm was exactly what you needed. Start practicing how to catch that critic (better known as "Bob") that looks up at the storm clouds and says, "This was really stupid."

### Reflection 46: Learning to Be Spontaneous and Honor Myself

For this exercise, write down three times of the day in your journal. Next, set alarms in your phone at those three times. It could be noon on Tuesday or three on Saturday. Then, when each alarm goes off, check in with yourself right away. The point is to tune in to yourself and then follow whatever your need or want is right then and there.

What are you feeling? What mood are you in? Ask yourself, *What would I like to do right now?* No judging. No, *But I have to do something else.* It could be something small, like getting a cup of coffee, as long as it's your need or your desire right at that very moment that you're making important.

Journal about what this exercise was like for you and keep it up. Have fun!

## Moving Toward Allowing Others to Take the Lead

Now it's time to address your tendency to take on too much responsibility. You're going to risk giving up control. Your new freedom will come from honoring yourself, your own time, or your own flagging energy level and say, "Enough is enough."

What discomfort will that bring? Again, it could be fear of how others view you. But the less obvious consequence may lie in a new sense of exposure or confusion. What if you actually have more time for you? You hide by being busy. Other uncomfortable results might be feelings of anger or disappointment if things aren't done by others the way you would've done them. Or you might find insecurity in your new role as onlooker—were you really needed in the first place? Were you appreciated?

You can see that with new risks come that onslaught of emotions we've discussed all along. But it's worth the risk, because it will also bring freedom of choice and freedom from so much heavy responsibility.

## Reflection 47: Choosing What I Want to Do with My Time

Choose three new behaviors to risk that will free up some of your time. Make decisions about what you *want* to do, not what you *need* or have to do. You might decide, *I'm going to give up being president of the board of the local food bank.* Or, *I'm not going to volunteer for the school holiday party, even if I have to sit on my hands.* (Remember Laura?) Or, *I will say no when I'm asked if I have time to spearhead the campaign.*

Learning what to do with all that extra time can be exhilarating and incredibly freeing. But you may have to remember or learn for the first time what it's like to relax and enjoy free time. Again, pick the one that would be easiest and go do it. Afterward, write out your results!

## Moving Toward Tolerance of Emotional Pain

The lesson here is to learn to stop discounting what hurt you in the past and what may be hurting you in the present. The goal is to label trauma, abuse, or neglect for what it was (or is still), while you increase your skills in knowing what to do with pain. For years, you've avoided it. Now it's time to trudge through it with self-compassion rather than shame.

Yes, this means sitting with feelings that are uncomfortable or unfamiliar. But I also invite you to think of other specific things that you can do to get closer to the pain you've had in your life, rather than pushing it away. It takes practice, but you can do it.

## Reflection 48: The Practice of Feeling Pain

This exercise is helpful in developing more self-compassion, the antidote for shame. First, get out photos of yourself at different ages. What do you remember about that age? Write about what you see or remember. Maybe show a friend or pin the pictures to your timeline.

Second, write a letter to yourself as that child. What could you say to them that you wished you'd known then? What did that child need to hear that they didn't? Often the answer to that last question is, "It wasn't your fault." It can also be very meaningful to have that child write back to you. What does that child need you to know about them? Try using your non-dominant hand for this second letter. (There are different theories about this approach, but one is that employing your brain's nondominant hemisphere may allow you to pull for other feelings or memories.) It can be amazing what emerges.

Third, going back and visiting the places where painful things occurred can also bring you closer to what hurt you. (Many of you may remember the scene in *Forrest Gump* when Jenny throws rocks at the prison that was her house, sobbing uncontrollably.) You can have someone go with you so that you're not alone.

Please be careful here. If you have the tendency to dissociate or have been diagnosed with post-traumatic stress disorder, this may not be safe to do, even with a friend. You'd need a trusted therapist to help guide you through such an experience.

You may be able to think of other actions that would help you walk through your pain, asking family or longtime friends questions, for example. But now is the time to decide what those things will be.

Order your proposed actions once again in what would be easiest to do, and then move to the more difficult, keeping in mind my warning about not going it alone if you're too disturbed by trauma. And as always, journal about your new experiences.

### Moving Toward Learning How to Feel Calm and Give Up Constant Worry

All of us, every day, cope with not knowing exactly what will happen in the next moment. If you tried to imagine and protect yourself and those you love from every potential mishap, your anxiety would go through the roof. Some of you may suffer from that very problem. Giving up the practice of worry, however, will be hard for you. *Worry is the way I feel in control. I'm anticipating what could go wrong and doing something about it.* When you say this to yourself, you're justifying the intensity of your worry. In actuality, worry is keeping you away from other emotions—and helping you stay in your head.

If you're struggling to curb your worry, I'll offer this analogy. Imagine that I'm holding a pen in my hand. First, I hold it as tightly as possible, my hand trembling with the force of my grasp. And then I switch. I hold it loosely, yet firmly. Which method exhausts me? The first. Which method leaves me free to respond in the moment if something were to occur? The second. That's what discovering calm will do for you.

### Reflection 49: Learning Skills to Build Calm

Now's the time to pick three things that you want to do to curb or normalize your worry. I'll offer some ideas. One technique is to start a separate worry journal; for this task, you sit down every day at the same time and write for ten minutes about everything you're worried about. Then put the journal aside and tell yourself, *I'm not going to worry any more about that until the same time tomorrow.* If you slip, get out your phone and write a note to yourself about the concern that came to you. But still put it away until tomorrow. Through this exercise, you want to both honor and corral your worry.

You can also look back to Reflection 4, "I believe that worry…," to see what you believed about worry. But remember, now you're focusing on action! You might decide, "I will buy a book on how to stop worrying." Or, "I'll tie a string around my finger to remind myself to not worry." Or, "Instead of worrying, I'll go find solid information." Or, "I'll download a meditation app today, get up twenty minutes early, and begin that practice in the morning." Make a commitment to yourself. Find your courage, breathe, and dig in.

### Moving Toward Enriching My Life with Creativity and Play

How long has it been since you've skipped down the sidewalk? Well, we're going to find out. Because here's where you can start to play and be creative. Accomplishment is something that can build esteem, but without balance it's a slave driver. So this list will be providing that balance. It's time to tell yourself, *I have done enough,* and move into, *I want to play, to have fun, to be creative—without any pressure or expectation.*

You may have intense discomfort with playing. You might think, *What will someone think if I'm at home not doing anything?* Or, *What will it look like if my friend sees me at a picnic when she knows I haven't finished my part of the project?* Or, *What if all I did today was paint?* Obviously, using your perfectionistic thinking, that would make you a loafer, a ne'er-do-well. It's that all-or-nothing, black-and-white thinking again.

### Reflection 50: Learning How to Play

Confront your critical thinking and move on to this next list. It'll be based on whatever it is you enjoy that's playful or creative or enjoyable. You might write, "I'll leave work thirty minutes early two times a week to make a yoga class." Or, "I'm going to get out my old piano books and play." Or, "I'm going to call a friend who always makes me laugh and plan something together."

Now you go! Write a list of ten things that you would like to do that are creative or playful. Then pick the one that would be the easiest and do it as soon as possible. I can't wait for you to discover, perhaps for the first time, the joy of playing. Write about what you discover along the way. And don't forget the skipping. It feels wonderful.

### Moving Toward Allowing Others into My Real World

Letting other people in so that they really know you is something you've not done. This is a chance for you to allow people who care about you to discover their own talent for giving. Allow your loved ones to know how good it can feel to be leaned on, to know that you value their opinion, or that your relationship with them can survive and thrive even given conflict.

In the final chapter, we'll talk more about the various reactions you might get when you open up and how to handle them. You might want to jump ahead and read what's offered there if you're not quite sure about opening up.

### Reflection 51: Opening Up

Pick three opportunities to open up. You might decide, *I'll choose to talk with my partner about something I would like to change in our relationship.* Or, *Today I'm going to talk to my supervisor about my mom's illness. It's been affecting my work, and I've been trying to cover it up.* Or, *I'm going to call the friend who saw me a few days ago and asked, "Are you okay?" I smiled and brushed her off. Today I'm going to tell her she was right—I'm not okay.*

Here's your chance to begin to learn to open up—today. Write about what you experience each time you reveal something about yourself. You can do this!

### Moving Toward Self-Compassion

You're more than halfway through the action steps! I hope you're getting excited about the changes you're making. You should be proud of yourself.

What are the skills tied to self-compassion? One is the skill of tuning in to yourself, checking how you're feeling physically, mentally, emotionally, and spiritually. And then allowing that information to matter—because you matter. You worked on this in a fun way when we talked about challenging your shaming voice and doing something in the moment, just for you. If you're tired or sick, if your mind is in a fog, if you're emotionally drained, if you're spiritually out of sync, then taking action to attend to yourself is crucial to being self-compassionate.

Of course, there are other parts of self-compassion: self-forgiveness and self-love, to name two. But again, we're focusing on action here. What can you do today that will build your skill at taking care of yourself in a much healthier way?

### Reflection 52: I Matter

Once again, please list three things that you can do in the next month that would be kind, caring things to do for yourself. It could be anything: a massage, going to the bookstore and hanging out, taking your first rock-climbing lesson. Anything that would nourish your spirit, mind, and body—that's where you want to head.

And then choose and go! Come back to your journal and record how you felt as you let yourself matter.

### Moving Toward Accepting and Managing My Health Issues

You've struggled to admit that you have other mental or physical health issues going on. You know you're worn down, but you tell yourself that's normal. You want to believe that you're simply having fun when you compulsively order things online. You eat "healthy," but you get your sense of worth from being the skinniest one in your friend group. You count on your pills to calm you down. But everyone does that, right?

Now's the time to realistically assess your own health. This will take objectivity on your part, and your unease may come roaring in at this point. It's vulnerable to go to a health care provider and be totally honest. You don't want the things that have kept you in control to be taken away or questioned. Now's when you need to listen to the voice that's fighting for your true well-being. Listen and see what it's telling you.

### Reflection 53: Taking Care of My Own Needs

Please list three things that you can do in the next month to take much better care of yourself in the long term. You're not looking for quick fixes. You want to pursue things that will establish a path toward wellness and health on all fronts.

Go for a wellness check and talk with your doctor honestly about pain or discomfort you might've been discounting. Make an appointment with a therapist. Look for a book or information on what's going on with your mind or body. Join a gym. Check in a with a spiritual counselor or mentor for guidance. Get more sleep. Make an appointment with a nutritionist, or simply eat better. The theme here is getting help for what is out of balance.

Write about what's difficult in turning the spotlight on your own needs. What do you feel when you do so?

## Moving Toward Honoring Both the Positive and the Negative

Gratitude and awareness can go hand in hand. You can count your blessings and admit the burden of struggles all at the same time. Your fear can be hard at work here, saying you have no right to complain, that you have to look resilient, that others might think less of you or think you're asking for pity. I could go on and on. And yet, with every choice, there are always pros and cons. Every situation has its upside and its downside.

Remember talking about a blessing's "underbelly"? That underbelly comes into play with thoughts such as, *I love my new job, and yet the commute is tough right now.* Or, *I'm excited I got the role in the play, but I'm not sure how I'm going to handle school.* Expressing the downside doesn't negate the positive of the upside. Even if you're complaining a little, so what? We all can do a little complaining from time to time.

The next reflection list is going to be a little different. I want you to experience not just your own awareness of something's downside. I want you to talk about it with several individuals in your friend group and discuss how to handle it. It will be interesting to hear their reaction. You may have chosen friends who do the same thing you do… and when you try to talk about the downside, they quickly want to turn the discussion back to the positive or want to stay focused on the solution, rather than allowing you to talk about your struggle. You can run your own experiment and see who in your friend group can actually hang out in the downside.

### Reflection 54: Hanging Out in the Downside

Pick three issues that you want to discuss, three downsides to your life, and three friends (or more) with whom you want to talk about it. You might decide, "I'll talk with Larry about how frustrating it is that, although I caught my shoulder injury before it got too bad, it's not healing from surgery." "I'll open up to Kindra about my kid getting on the competition soccer team, which is great, but I have no idea how we as a family are going to handle all that travel." Your goal is to have that conversation without shame.

Good luck! Afterward, write about the feelings you had in opening up.

### Moving Toward Building Vulnerability and Intimacy in Relationships

The entire last chapter of this book will be devoted to this topic. But you can certainly begin the process of identifying the relationships in which you're stuck solidly behind your mask. By inviting your spouse or a friend to join you in building on what you began in other reflections—becoming more vulnerable, letting them in on secrets, being able to admit when things get rough—you're moving toward combating the loneliness that you've had a hand in creating. Now you're also letting those you love know that you want to not just change yourself but to also deepen the intimacy between the two of you. You want that same kind of vulnerability reciprocated.

### Reflection 55: Risking True Intimacy

Now let's get started. Pick three ways that you keep people at a distance, no matter who they are. Next, decide what you're going to do to alter that behavior. For example, instead of saying "I'm fine" to everyone, decide you're going to tell at least one person more of the truth. Maybe that's the fact that you're having a really fantastic day. Or maybe you say, "You know, I'm a little under the weather. But I'm headed to the doctor to find out what's going on." In other words, you choose to share more of your true self and want others to do the same. You might decide, "I'm going to ask my wife to dinner and suggest that we don't talk about the kids—that I miss really knowing her."

Practicing these ten new directions is a huge beginning for you. You'll use this process over and over again to notice, identify, understand, and risk. Good for you that you've come this far! It's taken persistence and courage.

In the next chapter, we're going to focus on individual issues and triggers that may keep you from continuing on this journey. But you've achieved so much. Each step toward freedom and self-compassion feeds the good wolf and ensures that you're winning the battle.

# PART III

# Living Your True Self

# CHAPTER 4

# Growing into Your New Imperfect Skin

*When you first try to make a pot on a wheel, the clay does not obey your fingers. You end up with a wet, muddy mess. With practice, though, you become adept at handling clay in relation to the spin of the wheel and can create functional and beautiful things.*

—Stephen Batchelor, author of *Buddhism Without Beliefs*

We started Stage 5 with the need to grieve. I can't stress this enough. Once you begin to comprehend the cost of covering up for many years, the sadness and loss you feel can be overwhelming. But it's important to allow yourself to grieve. You're grieving the reason why you developed perfectly hidden depression. And you're grieving its impact on your life and the lives of others you care about. Try not to be afraid of grieving. Remember, if you've now uncovered what's been hiding depression, if you've begun to unveil your own feelings, you still have to deal with the depression itself.

One analogy for the therapy process that you might've heard is that it's like peeling an onion. There are layers upon layers of potential realizations, and each one of them can lead to a new level of awareness. This explanation may sound as if the psychology profession simply wants to keep itself in business. But that's not the case.

When you begin a journey of discovery, you're not sure how many layers lie within. It's the same with the *matryoshka* doll metaphor we discussed earlier—many dolls are enclosed within one doll, and it can be a surprise to learn how many are encased.

Stephen Batchelor (quoted above), in his book *Buddhism Without Beliefs*, points out that the attainment of awareness is messy and ever changing. "So what are we but the story we keep repeating, editing, censoring, and embellishing in our heads?... Instead of clinging to habitual behavior and routines as a means to secure this sense of self, we realize the freedom to create who we are" (1997, 82–83).

You're doing that now. You're discovering the fulfillment of creating who you are, how you want to grow, and what needs to be challenged to work through your depression.

In both the third and fifth stages of the five C's, we discussed moving toward certain directions—directions that involve a much greater sense of choice. In your journal, you listed different risks you want to take that would move you in that direction.

One of the reasons I use the term "moving toward," rather than "moving forward" or even "moving to," is to highlight the idea that risk and change are ongoing processes. You can choose at any time to stop. Yet each risk will bring with it a renewed sense of freedom and can invite you to consider another change, and another, and another. It's exciting. It can be scary. And it feels very alive.

In this chapter, we're going to focus on four things that might cause a derailment of this process as an individual. Much earlier, we focused on potential hurdles to committing to change in the first place. Now you've started and you're doing great. But what could lie around the corner that might cause a stall or a relapse into old perfectly hidden depression patterns?

- Confusion about or underestimation of certain psychiatric symptoms

- Defining slipups as failures rather than as part of the process

- Unconscious triggers

- Getting stuck in one stage of grief

Let's talk about each one.

## Confusion About or Underestimation of Certain Psychiatric Symptoms

Perfectionism itself can be found in many forms of anxiety, various eating disorders, and body image and self-esteem issues. But there are four psychiatric disorders that share several traits with perfectly hidden depression, other than depression itself. It's important that you don't minimize or discount these other psychiatric issues. Their presence could be essential to recognize and treat. Perfectly hidden depression, as I've stressed several times, isn't a diagnosis—it's a syndrome. Thus, mistakenly labeling these other psychiatric issues as solely "perfectly hidden depression" or underestimating their importance could hinder your growth and stability.

### Perfectly Hidden Depression vs. Bipolar II Disorder

First let's look briefly at bipolar II disorder. It's a cyclic disorder, meaning that you can experience frequent unexplained mood shifts, moving from being hyped up and full of energy into a more depressive episode. These shifts can happen at various rates. (I haven't included another form of bipolar disorder, bipolar I, due to the fact that its symptoms are more dramatic and thus not as likely to be discounted as due only to PHD.) So if you're someone who can get an incredible amount accomplished, have oodles of energy, have problems turning your mind off, struggle with anxiety, and don't sleep much, is that perfectly hidden depression or the more energetic stage of bipolar II disorder?

**Bipolar II disorder** must meet criteria for a current or past hypomanic episode *and* criteria for a current or past depressive episode, according to the *Diagnostic and Statistical Manual of Mental Disorders,* 5th edition (*DSM-5*; American Psychiatric Association 2013).

*Hypomania* is a distinct period of abnormally and persistently elevated, expansive, or irritable mood and abnormally and persistently increased activity or energy present most of the day for at least four consecutive days. A diagnosis of hypomania also includes at least three of the following symptoms:

- An inflated self-esteem or grandiosity

- A decreased need for sleep

- Being more talkative than usual or pressure to keep talking

- A flight of ideas or subjective experience of racing thoughts

- Distractibility

- An increase in goal-directed activity (socially, at work or school, or sexually) or physical agitation

- An excessive involvement in activities with high potential for painful consequences (e.g., buying sprees, foolish investments, sexual indiscretions)

A *depressive episode* is when five or more of the following symptoms are present during the same two-week period (and at least one of the symptoms must be either depressed mood or loss of interest or pleasure):

- Depressed mood most of the day, nearly every day

- Markedly diminished interest or pleasure in all or almost all activities

- Significant unintended weight loss or change in appetite

- Insomnia or hypersomnia

- Being physically agitated or listless

- Fatigue or loss of energy

- Feelings of worthlessness or excessive/inappropriate guilt

- Diminished ability to think or concentrate, or indecisiveness

- Recurrent thoughts of death, recurrent suicidal ideation, a suicide attempt, or a plan for suicide

Once again, my own life story lends some perspective. Around the time of my second divorce, I sought the help of a psychiatrist for panic attacks. Looking back on it, he wasn't very capable, especially as a therapist, and I didn't remain under his care for very long. He viewed my intense energetic work ethic (I was in graduate school), my (seeming) ability to focus and detach from emotional pain, and my ability to juggle fourteen balls at once as hypomania. He prescribed lithium, a mood-stabilizing drug. I dragged around for a week or two, practically comatose. The doctor was quite wrong. I didn't have hypomania. I was struggling with shame and grief, expertly covered up by perfectionism.

Intensely focusing on tasks getting done is part of your nature, and like me in graduate school, you might appear to be in overdrive. There's little relaxation or hang time in either perfectly hidden depression or the hypomanic stage of bipolar II. Yet, someone with bipolar II disorder may experience an over-the-top energy, tinged with anxiety and agitation, and then slide into a sadness or depression. The swing is noticeable to others and affects that person's daily functioning.

Those with perfectly hidden depression don't swing into obvious depression. Nor do they feel grandiose. Neither would be allowed.

If you identify with this cycle, then you need to talk with a mental health professional to determine these distinctions. Remember as well that you could identify with perfectly hidden depression and still have some bipolar II traits. Please educate yourself and seek help.

## Perfectly Hidden Depression and Anxiety Disorders

Most of us can easily reveal minor worries or anxieties. Maybe you're familiar with worries such as, "I'm nervous about this interview," or "I have to lose five pounds before we go to the beach." Yet a true anxiety disorder is much more burdensome. There are many types of anxiety disorders, but there are two that are important to discuss. One that shares a primary feature with perfectly hidden depression—worry—is generalized anxiety disorder (GAD).

People with severe generalized anxiety disorder can complain frequently of being able to visualize traumatic things happening. They may actually feel as if these visions are accurately predicting violence—that immense danger is not just a potential but a reality. It's as if they're watching a video that they don't know how to shut off. This very difficult problem is not part of the perfectly hidden depression syndrome.

> **Generalized anxiety disorder** is characterized by excessive anxiety or worry that occurs for more days than not for at least six months about a number of events or activities. According to the *DSM-5* (American Psychiatric Association 2013) it is also characterized by difficulty controlling the worry. For this diagnosis, the anxiety or worry must be associated with at least three of the following symptoms:
>
> - Restlessness or feeling on edge
> - Being easily fatigued
> - Difficulty concentrating or mind going blank
> - Irritability
> - Muscle tension
> - Sleep disturbance

What generalized anxiety disorder does share with perfectly hidden depression is the prevalence of worry.

Reid Wilson discusses the worry of GAD in his book *Don't Panic*: "With generalized anxiety disorder, panic is not the dominant feature… over 90 percent of them worry about minor events throughout the day… 'Will I fail in this work setting?' 'Are they going to accept me?' 'I'm afraid my kids are going to be harmed.' 'What if one day I can't pay the mortgage?... Those with generalized anxiety disorder focus more on their inability to cope with external events" (2009, 43–45).

Perhaps you can see a difference here between the worry of generalized anxiety disorder and the worry of perfectly hidden depression. In PHD, your worry is much more likely to be centered on the fear of exposure and the loss of control. You feel confident in your ability to handle stress or external pressures, unlike someone with generalized anxiety disorder. In fact, it's what you seem to do perfectly.

There's another important difference between generalized anxiety disorder and perfectly hidden depression.

Please again take a quick look at the symptoms of GAD. In perfectly hidden depression, you hide your anxiety as best you can and look as if you're coping very well. As Lacey put it, "I might be worried, but I'd look to others as if I had things in the bag." Someone with generalized anxiety disorder can't hide their anxiety from the world; they're known as worriers or may constantly advise their children of danger. Worry invades their thinking to the point that they often struggle to function and may even isolate themselves from the world.

We've also talked before about the likelihood that someone who experiences perfectly hidden depression may also have traits of obsessive-compulsive disorder (OCD), another type of anxiety disorder.

**Obsessive-compulsive disorder** is characterized by the presence of obsessions, compulsions, or both. The obsessions or compulsions are time-consuming (i.e., take more than one hour per day) or cause clinically significant distress or impairment in social, occupational, or other important areas of functioning.

As defined by the *DSM-5* (American Psychiatric Association 2013), *obsessions* are recurrent and persistent thoughts, urges, or images that are experienced as intrusive and unwanted, and, in most individuals, cause marked anxiety or distress. Those with OCD attempt to ignore or suppress such thoughts, urges, or images, or to neutralize them with some other thought or action (i.e., by performing a compulsion).

*Compulsions* are repetitive behaviors (e.g., hand washing, ordering, checking) or mental acts (e.g., praying, counting, silently repeating words) that the individual feels driven to perform in response to an obsession or according to rules that must be applied rigidly. The behaviors or mental acts are aimed at preventing or reducing anxiety or distress, or preventing some dreaded event or situation. However, they're not connected in a realistic way with what they are designed to neutralize or prevent, or they are clearly excessive.

Obsessive-compulsive disorder reflects a compulsive need to do certain things in an attempt to control anxiety. If you have OCD, you may, for example, consistently need to make lists for everything, have repetitive rituals that you're compelled to do, struggle with being flexible, count objects around you obsessively, or have to have your surroundings so scrupulously clean that you're up at 2:00 a.m. mopping the kitchen floor.

Brittany, who strongly identified with perfectly hidden depression but also had some OCD traits, felt compelled to keep a highly detailed daily calendar. It was so jam-packed, filled with Post-it notes and tabs, that it was almost indecipherable to anyone else. She was embarrassed to show it to me and worked on "cleaning it up" before she did. The intense level of her own required precision was sad to see, but she found the ritual of keeping such meticulous lists comforting.

Again, talking with a mental health professional about both generalized anxiety disorder and obsessive-compulsive disorder might clear up these distinctions for you. As with bipolar II, it may not be an either/or situation but an "and." The goal is for you to understand your struggles as clearly as possible, and it can be helpful to rule out these conditions. You're not borrowing trouble. You're making sure you understand and receive the help you need.

### Perfectly Hidden Depression vs. Borderline Personality Disorder

One of the chief characteristics of borderline personality disorder (BPD) is a life ruled by intense, impulsive, and unstable emotions. Those who have BPD have lives filled with emotional chaos, lots of dramatic ups and downs, self-destructive tendencies, suicide attempts, and an immense fear of abandonment.

**Borderline personality disorder** is characterized by a pervasive pattern of instability of interpersonal relationships, self-image, and affects, according to the *DSM-5* (American Psychiatric Association 2013). It's also marked by impulsivity, beginning by early adulthood and present in a variety of contexts, as indicated by five or more of the following symptoms:

- Frantic efforts to avoid real or imagined abandonment
- A pattern of unstable and intense interpersonal relationships characterized by alternating between extremes of idealization and devaluation
- Identity disturbance: markedly and persistently unstable self-image or sense of self
- Impulsivity in at least two areas that are potentially self-damaging (e.g., spending, sex, substance abuse, reckless driving, binge eating)
- Recurrent suicidal behavior, gestures, or threats, or self-mutilating behavior
- Affective instability due to a marked reactivity of mood (e.g., intense episodic dysphoria, irritability, or anxiety usually lasting a few hours and only rarely more than a few days)
- Chronic feelings of emptiness
- Inappropriate, intense anger or difficulty controlling anger
- Transient, stress-related paranoid ideation or severe dissociative symptoms

So why would someone with borderline personality disorder identify with perfectly hidden depression? From my work with patients with BPD, they often describe feeling as if there's a dark, very empty part of themselves, a part that's ultimately filled with despair, loneliness, self-loathing, or rage. One patient called it "a black hole that tries to suck any goodness out of my life." This dark, empty part of themselves can overlap with or seem similar to the "hidden self" of perfectly hidden depression. Another patient with

BPD said, "Perfectly hidden depression is exactly how I feel. I hide all the time. I can be two people at once."

In her outstanding book on mothers with BPD, *Understanding the Borderline Mother*, Christine Ann Lawson describes this borderline duality. She states that recognizing someone with borderline personality disorder can be difficult because they can seem normal in nonintimate relationships, they have "different external or public personalities," and they "function well in structured environments and in specific roles" (2000, 37). Some of this sounds very similar to perfectly hidden depression.

But what drives behavior is quite different between them. In fact, the dynamics of perfectly hidden depression and borderline personality disorder could be considered as being on opposing emotional poles. In PHD, intellectualization and overanalyzing tightly rule behavior, whereas dramatic emotions and impulsivity rule someone with BPD.

Both sadly and happily, they're not the same. If you see yourself in the criteria for borderline personality disorder, it's essential that you seek help. There are specific treatment regimens, such as dialectical behavior therapy, that can be highly effective; with hard work, you can develop a more stable life.

### Reflection 56: Do I Need to Consider That I May Have One of These Disorders?

Upon reading about the disorders that share features with perfectly hidden depression, you might be tempted to think, *Oh, I do that.* Or, *Gosh, I've felt that way before.* Many of us have bursts of energy at times; many of us may find it hard to corral worry or are afraid of being lonely. If your emotions get too involved, you can make the mistake of pathologizing things about you that almost all of us do and that are normal.

Instead, try looking at these criteria and your behavior as objectively as you can. Write out if you've identified with any of these separate diagnostic categories. And then, if you feel it's a good idea, make an appointment with your family doctor, a psychiatrist, or a therapist—someone with whom you can discuss your symptoms objectively. You don't want to make the mistake of not paying attention. But you also don't want to hyperanalyze everything so that you unintentionally ramp up concern where it doesn't need to exist. You simply want to make sure that you're covering all bases. If you're struggling with an actual psychiatric condition, this information can guide your choices.

## Defining Slipups as Failure Rather Than Part of the Process

I've stated many times that unfamiliar pain is much more frightening than familiar pain. When you risk doing something "unlike" you, when you try on a new behavior, that risk will bring discomfort. After all, perfectly hidden depression may have worked pretty darn well—until it didn't. So choosing discomfort may be hard.

As a therapist, I've watched people try to change their lives in many different ways. Often, those efforts will be going quite well, and then...bam! You're caught by surprise, not knowing exactly what to do. Your stress level is so high that you turn to what's old hat—to that familiar (even if unhealthy) coping strategy. This partially explains why recovering alcoholics with years of sobriety under their belt relapse. Or how couples who've learned healthier communication skills deteriorate into old patterns when they have an extensive visit from family over the holidays. Or why your healthier eating plan was going really, really well, until one of your children has to go into the hospital and out comes your favorite comfort food. We all do it—or it takes an inordinate amount of self-discipline and self-awareness not to do it.

When you realize you've "relapsed," you can beat yourself up and feel helpless about maintaining your intention. Or you can realize that it's part of the process.

It's essential to accept that you're not failing when you fall back into old choices or patterns. You're learning. And part of learning is making mistakes. Your intention and commitment can be renewed as many times as necessary.

I want to repeat this. Part of healthy learning is slipping up. Part of healthy learning is making mistakes. Part of healthy learning is having compassion for yourself when you go back on automatic pilot. It takes time to establish a new normal. Remember, your focus is on the journey, not the destination.

Then let's not forget the role of shame ("Bob" again). It can so easily lift up its voice, sneering, "You see, I told you reading this wasn't going to help… Who did you think you were fooling? You might as well give up now."

Allow yourself to renew your intention with every slipup and you'll stay the course. Shame yourself and you'll be back trying to look perfect again.

## The Power of Unconscious Triggers

Inextricably tied up with slipping, going back on autopilot, and desperately wanting to hide even after you recognize the importance of growing comfortable with vulnerability are *triggers*.

What is a trigger? Here's an example.

*Margaret's Story:* Triggered by Golf

*One Saturday morning when my son was a toddler, my husband quite innocently stood in the kitchen and wondered aloud, "Would I like to play golf today?"*

*What's important to know is he'd been on the golf course maybe twice since our son was born. He'd change diapers and take feedings and do everything he could do to be a great dad. Not Superman, but a great dad. So when I exploded right then and there, both of us were shocked.*

*"What do you mean you want to go play golf?" I yelled.*

*He looked stunned. I was stunned. Tears came immediately into my eyes. I couldn't blame it on hormones, that's for sure. My son was two.*

*Quite suddenly, I remembered something I hadn't thought of in years. My dad had been an avid golfer and would often*

*take the few Saturdays he had off to play. And I was left at*
*home with my mom, who, sadly but frequently, confided way*
*too much in me about their relationship.*

   *Very well-hidden, very old anger about that whole dynamic*
*came roaring out of me that Saturday morning like a freight*
*train headed down a mountain.*

At that moment, what had been largely unconscious came dramatically into my conscious mind. A trigger reflects that something has power for you today because of its association with the past.

### Conscious Triggers

We all have emotional or mental triggers, many of which are known to us. Those are conscious. Some of them are pleasant. You smell pipe smoke and remember your beloved granddad. You get sentimental as you take out holiday decorations, associating different ones with various vacations or family rituals.

But many conscious triggers definitely aren't pleasant. The scratchiness of a beard on your face brings back memories of your sexual abuser. Hearing a semi traveling in the next lane causes anxiety because of a previous car wreck. At their worst, triggers themselves can cause flashbacks, which in turn cause you to feel as if you're experiencing the trauma of the past all over again. A car backfiring becomes gunfire and you hit the floor. You see the same kind of dog that viciously attacked you years ago and you run away, terrified.

### Unconscious Triggers

Then there are triggers that we don't know about consciously. Remember Mallory? She'd been neglected most of the time as a child. When she did get attention, it was either highly critical or an onslaught of over-the-top rushes of endearment. It had been confusing to her and she'd found safety in isolation. She'd not experienced warm, consistent love from a parent. Much later in her life, when her own children wanted her to be close with them, she felt weirdly trapped and fought old feelings of needing to get away. She was getting triggered. Her timeline helped her see this trigger and the connection between present and past.

Dial back for a minute to your earlier work with connecting with emotions. You designed a timeline. You wrote out the messages you'd received from each event. You connected with the emotion of that message and then began the work of identifying any patterns between your behavior now and the past events on your timeline.

Discovering unconscious triggers is a continuation of that work. So how do you know you're being unconsciously triggered? Typically, you're either overreacting or underreacting to something. Your reaction doesn't objectively "fit" the situation. That's when you can perceive the kernel (either positive or painful) of an earlier experience.

It's your reaction that's the clue.

Perhaps you were emotionally abused as a child, so you don't see your girlfriend's manipulation as manipulation: you underreact. Or maybe you were raged at as a child, so when your best friend reveals he's angry with you, you jump to the conclusion that he's ending the friendship: you overreact.

### Blatant vs. Subtle Triggers

Triggers can be blatant or they can be subtle. For example, if a tornado ripped through your childhood home, you're likely terrified of tornadoes and get extremely emotional when one is close by. That's a blatant and conscious trigger.

Janessa's story will help us understand more subtle triggers that can keep old, unhealthy patterns alive and well.

#### *Janessa's Story:* Struggling to See Triggers

*Janessa had been a happy-go-lucky teenager and couldn't wait to get to college to see what lay in store for her future. She came from a family of strong, adventurous women who were known for their tenacity.*

One night, when walking down a dark, more remote part of campus, she was violently raped. She told no one but her parents. Her attacker wore a ski mask, so she couldn't have recognized him in a lineup. Like many victims, she never reported the rape. She went home for a long weekend and then went back to school. She distanced herself as much from the trauma as she could and "put it behind her."

Only when I directly asked a question about sexual abuse was it even mentioned. She told me she never thought about it anymore. When asked how it had changed her, she said, "I don't think it did." She had no problem with sexual intercourse and dismissed it.

She came in and out of therapy several times. The theme was always the same: She kept being attracted to men who lied to and manipulated her. She kept all of their bad behavior a secret from her family and friends, acting as if everything was great. She was rising in the corporate ranks and was very successful. She used the stress of her job as a reason why she forgave—it was too much trouble to find someone else. When she'd finally get enough of one guy and break up, she'd find another one who treated her poorly.

Over the years, I suggested several times that her awareness of and respect for her own emotional safety seemed minimal, and that her underreaction to lies and cheating might have a lot to do with the horror and the helplessness of the rape. She'd look at me blankly and say, "No, that's not it." We'd discussed family dynamics, problems with intimacy, and self-esteem struggles as possible contenders for what was leading to this self-sabotage. She'd make some progress. Yet just as when she'd shut down her feelings about her rape, when she discovered one more manipulation or one more lie, she'd go numb and become paralyzed.

I wasn't absolutely sure I was right. But it was the one piece of work she steadfastly refused to do. And her behavior in the present stayed the same.

Janessa's story illustrates how admitting and accepting that something is a trigger for you, whether you tend to be overreactive or underreactive, isn't as easy as it may sound.

### Reflection 57: Do I Know My Triggers?

Take out that now very familiar journal and allow yourself to remember the last time you realized you'd overreacted or underreacted to something. This takes a lot of objectivity about yourself, and you may need to ask your trusted buddy to help you with this one. They may be able to help you recognize when you discount something that others don't or when you get angry when there's no obvious reason for it.

Once you have described the situation, write about the possible trigger for that over- or underreaction. Look back at your timeline and see if there are events or experiences that could be the source of your triggered emotions. Ask yourself, *When have I felt this way before?*

During the next few days, try to be mindful of your reactions. Try to notice whether you're getting triggered, whether you're overreacting or underreacting. If you are, jot down what's going on in that moment. Then see where it might be connected to something from your past. Use your timeline for ideas. You might ask yourself, *Why did I get so embarrassed?* Or, *What's going on that I didn't even notice she was crying?* It takes practice, but you can get quite good at this!

Let's talk again about *trauma*, which is a highly distressing or disturbing experience that evokes feelings of deep vulnerability. It's often the source of triggers. As you worked on your timeline, you may very well have discovered traumatic experiences. Or as you recognize more and more what your triggers are, you may come to label something as traumatic that previously you discounted or even denied.

Healing from trauma is painstaking. If you're now realizing that you experienced some kind of trauma, whether it was sexual or physical, developmental or relational, then seeing a therapist who's been trained in working with trauma is the safest and best way to heal. That's not about weakness on your part. That's about the intensity of the damage done. Specific techniques such as hypnosis and eye movement desensitization and reprocessing (EMDR) can be used, as well as other approaches. You can ask your therapist which one might be best for you.

**Reflection 58:** Trauma in My Life

Return now to the timeline that you created and look through it once again. Begin to label as "trauma" any experience that was deeply distressing and evokes feelings of vulnerability.

You may flinch at the thought of calling something "trauma," just as you had to become accustomed to the word "abuse." But ask yourself, *If this had happened to someone I love, would I see it as traumatic for them?* If the answer is yes, label it so.

That said, you may not have any trauma in your background. However, a lot of you will, and hopefully you can begin to realize and connect with the damage of those experiences with compassion.

## Getting Stuck in One Stage of Grief

At the beginning of this chapter, I again stressed the need for grieving. But there can be a hitch. You can get stuck in one stage or another. The classic stages, initially defined by Elisabeth Kübler-Ross in *On Death and Dying* (2014), are denial, anger, bargaining, depression, and acceptance. The process isn't fixed, like a worm turning into a butterfly. The stages don't follow a set path. Emptiness, agitation, disbelief, sadness, a sense of abandonment, and other complex feelings of grief can swirl around you, coming and going randomly.

In some ways, identifying with perfectly hidden depression may mean that you've been stuck in one stage of grief for quite some time—the stage of denial. As you move out of that denial, many other emotions are waiting for you. And they can be overpowering. You don't want to get stuck in one of the other stages, however, no matter how consuming those feelings can be. But if day after day you're angry, or day after day your sadness consumes you, then you may be getting stuck.

It's important to safely express those feelings as much as you need, and for as long as is helpful. But these feelings need to go and come, not entrench themselves into your everyday life. (You might want to return to Stage 4 and review the techniques we outlined there.)

### Reflection 59: Assessing My Grief

Consider for a moment something that you know you've grieved. Then write about how you went through the different stages of grief. It could be helpful, if you struggle to look at yourself in this way, to describe the stages that someone you know well went through. Did you or they get stuck in any one stage? Did you or they avoid any of the stages? If so, how might you want to do it differently now?

In the next and final chapter, we'll discuss how the people in your world may respond to these changes in you, and how you can work with them to try to ensure that you stay on the path of healing. In many ways, your change may be most obvious within your relationships. You've done an astounding job. Let's go forward now and focus on relationships.

# CHAPTER 5

# Breaking the Silence and Discovering a Happier Life

*If we can see it is our agreements that rule our own life, and we don't like the dream of our life, we need to change the agreements.*

—Don Miguel Ruiz, author of *The Four Agreements*

So far, we've focused on changes within you—changes that have allowed much more emotional freedom and that have challenged strategies and rules that no longer need to be followed.

But what about breaking the silence of perfectly hidden depression and beginning to invite others to get to know the new imperfect you? Along the way, I've asked you to involve others as you felt comfortable. I've encouraged you to share your path with at least one trusted friend. And whatever risks you chose to take in Stage 5 likely required more direct and honest communication with others.

In the stories that you've read about those with perfectly hidden depression, you've also seen how dramatic change occurred in their relationships as a result of their decisions to break their silence. You might now be wondering how your own partners, friends, and family will respond to the new "you."

A few of you may have taken the bull by the horns and forged ahead. If so, that's wonderful and I hope you've experienced the benefits of deepening that relationship.

But for many of you, these relationship changes may have remained in your imagination. Why? Because they can definitely be the scariest to make. When you start to let go and open up, you're inviting someone else into what has been your very private world. You can feel anxious and exposed. Even though you're sharing with people you love, or people who've been close to you (or as close as you've let anyone become), you can still be hesitant. Because while you're describing your own fresh revelations, you're also inviting change in the relationship. You may be quite nervous but also eager to see if your relationships can travel in a similar direction as you— becoming more open, more spontaneous, and more accepting of imperfection.

Especially with your partner, you may hope that they're able to meet you somewhere in the middle and communicate in a more real way. You want to create a kind of intimacy that you've never enjoyed. You want to be loved and accepted the way you are. You want true happiness. No secrets. No hiding.

Yet here can come that shameful voice, screaming at you that you don't have the right to ask others for anything, let alone that they consider a change in the relationship they have with you. How will they respond? What is the actual potential within the relationship for change? What if it can't occur? If you listen to that shame, it can keep you in fear.

There's also another problem. What if some of the people in your circles were an unintentional or, even worse, intentional part of a painful past that led you to create the facade of perfectionism? Or what if they've been a strong part of enabling you now? How are they going to respond to your new insights and real emotions? Changes in these relationships can run up against a lot of resistance or simply be impossible. On the other hand, it may not happen; you may fear it and it never occurs (as we saw in Spencer's story). But if it does, it can be very disappointing.

You want and need to create relationships in which you can be real. Whether you're a teenager or a thirtysomething or a fiftysomething, if there's one point I've tried to make in this book, it's that this work might save your life—not simply emotionally but your very life. Reaching out, choosing who you can trust, and risking opening up to them is paramount to not only healing but also to moving away from the dark thoughts that can come to those lost in loneliness and hopelessness. And as you read earlier, if you're under eighteen and in these circumstances, if your fear of opening up to your parents is too great, please look for an adult you can trust—a relative, a friend's parent, a teacher, a counselor—who can listen and help.

Consider the quote at the beginning of this chapter. Don Miguel Ruiz points out that you have the right to be who you are and ask for what you need and want. Just because you're living by a certain agreement or understanding now doesn't mean it can't or shouldn't change.

In this final chapter, it's time to discuss how you'll open up about your own journey and hope that your primary relationships can change. Recall Reflection 6, where you drew your inner circle—people who knew you the best or who were the closest to doing so. The circles widened as you began considering who else was important to you in your world. The closer people are to you in these circles, the more change you're likely to desire in that relationship.

Yet, like watching a fireworks display, what can start out as a tiny burst of color can spread and fill the entire sky in a gorgeous array of light. Change in one relationship can bolster your realization of how powerful and joyful it can be to let go of shame and live in self-acceptance. That realization can lead to risking change in another relationship, then another, and then another.

Let's look at how that process can happen. When I began blogging back in 2012, I believed I'd been quite honest in my relationships. I talked openly about my issues—or so I thought. In fact, the entire reason for creating my first website was to share all the nitty-gritty, emotional details of my adjustment to an empty nest. My only son had left for college in another state. And boom. The silence was at times too much to take. Gone was his youthful energy that I adored. There were pros. I could see the floor of his room for the first time in years. But I was a mess at first. In my blog I revealed intimate things, such as when I was huddled into a fetal position in the front seat of his car, crying my eyes out. What could be more open than that?

As I continued to write, those closest to me began seeing and hearing other changes in me. It didn't take me as long to process something. I wasn't as cautious. And the longer I've written, and the more I've challenged previous means of controlling my emotions, the more relaxed and open I've become. That initial year of blogging was my first fireworks. And the light spread into more and more of my life.

It was interesting to see how it affected my relationships. This change in me, for my friends who could also be open and vulnerable, was more than welcome. Yet from others I heard things like, "Are you sure you want to be that open on social media? Aren't you a little nervous about how you'll be perceived?"

You may also find that as these changes take root, and you discover how much happier and more relaxed you feel while also being productive and competent, you'll attract more of that kind of energy into your life. More people will sense the changes in you and be ready and willing to share their inner vulnerabilities with you as well.

Let's focus for a moment on the various responses you might receive from those you approach about your own change and healing. Whether they are a spouse or partner, friend or colleague, parent or other family member, the transition can go smoothly. But not always.

## Potential Responses to Relationship Change

Josie, who had made incredible progress on her perfectly hidden depression, told her family one day, "You're going to see some changes in me. So get ready. I'm going to do a better job of taking care of myself. I'm going to say no more often."

Her oldest son humorously responded, "That's great, Mom. Would you please do that with everyone but me?"

This is one amusing example of how your change may be accepted. But entire books could be written about how to handle the potential changes in your relationships as a result of you discovering and revealing yourself. We have a mere chapter. So let's cover the basic points.

## Embracing the Change

Many of those in your world may readily embrace the changes in you and respond in kind. Those who truly want the best for you will welcome what you slowly begin to reveal. Partners and friends may have watched with great concern as you took on more and more projects, rarely seemed to slow down and breathe, or never talked about what was going on in your own heart and mind. They may have felt your love but also felt shut out, suddenly cut off if they got too close.

## Reflection 60: Preparing to No Longer Stay Silent

Take a moment to think of how you might want to approach your partner or a friend. You can write out what you want to say and how you want to say it. As you did earlier, you can practice it out loud, as if you were going to give a speech or had a role in a play. Practicing like this can help you visualize the other person's reaction, which is likely to be similar to other experiences you've had with them. What will it feel like to be real?

What's important to remember is that even positive change in relationships can be stressful. And we all have our most comfortable and familiar strategy for handling stress, whether it's healthy or unhealthy. For the folks who can hear you and are overjoyed that you're opening up, their response will likely be welcome acceptance; they will wait to absorb this new information and ask what they can do to help you and build your relationship into a much stronger, better one. That's obviously what you're hoping for.

As your partner or your friend begins to understand more of what you're saying, their response can become even more secure and healthy. Remember, there's much about you they don't know, as you've kept your more painful memories locked away. As they become more comfortable with new information about you, as they begin to put the pieces together in their own understanding, as they begin to feel more comfortable with increasing their own vulnerability, they'll be more than willing to build a new normal with you.

If you've been suicidal, please know that that information can be very difficult to hear. You may need to reassure even the calmest of people that you're getting the help and support you need.

### Pushback

Yet there can be problems in sharing—problems that you can prepare for so as to not overreact. Choosing someone who'd rarely take the time or make the effort to know you more deeply or intimately could've seemed the perfect choice for a partner in the past. If that's what you've done, you may get pushback when you talk about wanting a deeper, more real connection. Let's focus briefly on three common relationship patterns that you may have inadvertently created.

First, the two of you may have been acting out what's called an approach/avoidant dynamic. They emotionally sought you out: they approached, sometimes in anger or disappointment, sometimes in love and tenderness. And the more they approached, the more you avoided, which only served to ramp up their approach into an even more intense emotional stance. You beginning to open up may be something they've desired for a long time. But they also may have become accustomed to doing the approaching and not quite know what to do when the roles are changed. This dynamic is one of the easier to identify; with a growing recognition on both parts, it's very workable—if resentments haven't festered and responsibility is taken on both sides for problems created.

Second, you may have created a dynamic whereby most of the giving has been from you to your partner. You may have settled for what you could get and basically overfunctioned in the relationship. And they've underfunctioned. They've walked through the relationship, accepting what you had to offer and not worked on their own emotional maturity or sense of responsibility for creating a healthy relationship. An even more difficult scenario occurs if the receiver has a pattern of manipulation or abuse, or suffers from narcissism or other destructive personality traits. This can be difficult to assess when you're intimately involved.

Third, you might've chosen someone who avoids conflict and likes emotions tucked away, out of sight. The two of you don't fight or rarely argue. They may be very much like you were and prefer things to remain emotionally neutral. You've functioned well as a team but haven't shared on an intimate level. Maybe you've lived separate lives in many ways—except when you both show up at community functions looking like the perfect couple.

Change in any of these relationship dynamics can be difficult and may not be possible on your own. If that's the case, please find a therapist who's knowledgeable about couples counseling.

These patterns may not stop with only your partner. Perhaps you've surrounded yourself with friends for whom superficiality has been the norm. And, of course, as we discussed previously, you may have come from a family that refused to discuss anything painful or unpleasant. Or that ridiculed you for doing so. You've talked more about common or "acceptable" stuff with them, such as problems with your kid's teacher or who won the ball game. But to reveal that you've thought about suicide? Or that you have sexual problems? Or that you're afraid your child might be depressed? Those much more revealing conversations have never taken place.

On the more optimistic side, you may find that if you open up just a bit, one of those "superficial" friends may quietly share, "I can't believe I'm telling you this, but I've felt the same way." Or, "I've been on an antidepressant for two years." Even your partner may hesitate but in the end say, "I haven't been all that happy either. Let's give this a try." Opening up can be a huge breath of fresh air in what have been stagnant relationships.

On the other side, your partner, your family, or your friends may have more defensive, knee-jerk reactions that might be unwelcome or harsh. And their impact on a very vulnerable, sensitive you could be confusing and painful. What you want to avoid is retreating inward and once again hiding. You may have to give others time to become more comfortable with this new you, realizing that a more fearful reaction is, hopefully, temporary—and that with time they'll respond more thoughtfully.

For clarity, let's divide potential negative reactions into the four well-known responses to fear: fight, flight, freeze, or fold.

### Fight

One fear response is to fight. It's active resistance. People responding in this mode may say, "I don't want to change my life. I'm happy with you the way things are." Or, "I don't want to sit around and talk about painful things. Why would you want to do that? We've always agreed to stay positive." They might turn things around and perceive your previous hiding as active deception, asking, "Why didn't you tell me this before? Did you not trust me? What other things are you hiding from me?"

There's also a more passive resistance within the fight response. Folks reacting in this way might nod their head as they listen, as if in total agreement with what is being asked of them. But underneath that facade, they have no intention of doing anything. When it's time to sit down and have that heart-to-heart conversation, they make excuses: "I thought I'd have time this afternoon, but things got away from me." Or, "Gosh, I've been through a hard, long day and just don't have the energy. Let's do it tomorrow." And tomorrow never comes.

### Flight

The flight response is exactly what it sounds like: escape. The proposed change to the relationship may be too frightening, and your partner or friend may feel very threatened—so threatened that they can withdraw and refuse to see it from your perspective. They might say, "I didn't know this was going on. I don't even know what to say." And then they leave. And they don't bring it up again.

Flight can also occur through denial, as they "escape" by denying that there's a problem. Perhaps they say flatly, "I don't believe that you've been depressed. You'd be sleeping all the time if you were. And you're the Energizer Bunny. Who's given you these ideas?" Your revelations are dismissed. And the opportunity for change is missed.

### Freeze

Think of a deer in the headlights and you'll be able to recognize the freeze response to fear. The animal stays quite still and quiet, assessing the danger to see if fleeing is necessary or whether it can go back to eating grass.

Similar to passive resistance, your partner may act as if they're listening. But in reality, they're hoping it will all go away so the status quo remains. (Sounds like something an underfunctioner might do...) Or they can say to themselves (probably not to you), "She gets like this sometimes. Tomorrow things will be the way they've always been." So they stay quiet. How does it differ from passive resistance? You're ignored more than resisted. When you try to bring it up again, it's as if you've never said anything before. No response, so nothing happens. But remember that doing absolutely nothing is a message in and of itself.

### Fold

Then there's a fold response whereby the fear is so devastating to someone that they lose some of their capacity to function. They feel emotionally overwhelmed by what you're saying and need a lot of reassurance from you that everything is okay. They may even shame themselves for what has been your journey. They might say, "I should've known how unhappy you've been." Or, "Did I make you feel this way?" This can be difficult because you don't want to revert to hiding who you are.

**Reflection 61:** My Responses to Fear

It may be helpful to journal about your own responses to fear. Do you stay calm? Or which one of the four reactions applies to you? This is important to know, because risking change is frightening. Recognizing your own reaction style will give you a heads-up when attempting to keep yourself emotionally balanced as you're risking change with your partner, friend, or family member.

You might also want to spend some time writing about how you predict each person will react. As previously mentioned, their reaction is likely going to be similar to what it's been in the past, so you can use that information to guide you. Why is this helpful? You may be less likely to feel hurt by a more fear-based response if you expect it. You can remain more objective and see their reaction as predictable, not personal.

So, what do you do if you receive one of these more difficult reactions? You hang on tight to your own boundaries. No matter what the reaction, it's vital to keep your boundaries very clear.

## Healthy Boundaries

What's a healthy boundary? If you share a healthy boundary with someone, you know that how you feel when you're with them comes from your own inner life, your own thoughts and feelings. The other person hasn't caused them. It's the conceptual line between where you end and someone else begins. You believe, *You didn't make me feel sad. I simply feel sad.*

But a boundary can also be defined in a very pragmatic way. You set a boundary when you establish guidelines for what is a permissible or safe way for others to act toward you, and what you'll likely do or feel if that line is crossed. "I'm going to close the door if you continue making so much noise in the kitchen" is a simple example. You can state your own personal boundaries, which provides structure for your own behavior. "I'll leave the room if I get too mad. But this conversation is important and I'll be back when I can cool down."

When boundaries are clear, they give information to others about who you are and what you care about. And vice versa. Just as important, they provide you with a sense of self. You assert what's important to you. You explain your values. You know what's motivating your decisions and guiding your emotional reactions.

Healthy boundaries aren't ultimatums, although you can be accused of that when they are unwelcome. They are information. That distinction is important to remember.

Keep in mind that it took you some time to allow your own thinking to change. And you can be generous with your partner, friend, or family member and give them that same time. You can invite them to ask you questions. But the boundary should be clear: "If you cannot try to change *with* me right now, I understand. But I'm going to continue this journey."

You can ask them if you can give some feedback on their reaction. You might say, "I'd like to talk about your anger with me." Or, "I'd like to talk about how I'm seeing the situation between us right now. You don't seem comfortable with what I've told you." You're encouraging a conversation that could be very helpful.

What your partner or friend may not realize is that they're giving you information through their reactions. If they remain angry, that's information for you to process. If they say, "You know, at first I got angry because I was caught off guard. I'm sorry I got defensive. Can we try this conversation over?" then that's a helpful response. If they blame themselves, that's information. Or if they say, "You know, I realize it's not about me. I just got scared," that helps you both move forward. If they continue to deny what you've said, then that's information. But if they say, "At first, I didn't want to believe that you've been depressed. That scared me. I don't know how to help you," then that's obvious progress. And they're also choosing increased vulnerability.

By considering their reaction as information, you can try to stay out of your own fearful or defensive reactions. You might have thoughts such as, *What if they don't ever want to talk about it?* Or, *What if they expect me to be my old perfect-looking self?* You can feel sad if it's going to be a harder journey than you expected. But your own alarm—your own fear—won't be helpful.

Evaluating someone's response as information allows you to more objectively assess their capability to grow with you. If they can, then it's absolutely wonderful. If they cannot, then you have to process that as well.

Anyone still following previous rules that you were following (that you now see as dysfunctional)—whether it's because of cultural or family beliefs—may not be capable of considering change. They may not understand how that belief system has been destructive for you. This becomes something you have to grieve. But it can be a relief as well. It's not your job to bring them along with you. It's your job to heal yourself.

Let's talk a little more about *capability*. Incapability doesn't equate with withholding. You'd never go to a hardware store and expect to buy ice cream. Sometimes people aren't withholding something from you; they don't have it to give. Here's another example: If I'm thirsty and I know you have water (you are capable of giving it to me), but you don't offer me a drink, I can see clearly that you're withholding it from me. My reaction might vary from anger to desperation to sadness. But if I'm thirsty and I can see that you have no water to give, although I wish that you did, I'll have a different reaction. In the latter case, you eventually need to accept the fact that, at this moment, they aren't capable of giving you what you desire. Then you can decide where your boundaries are and act on them.

If you hang in there, give your loved one time and space to consider what you're asking, then perhaps they'll also work toward a more intimate relationship—if they are capable—one that will support honesty, openness, and vulnerability.

Chase's story provides an interesting view of how widespread the change can be when you're no longer hiding.

*Chase's Story:* A Man Blossoming into a New Definition of Himself

*Chase entered therapy because he was distraught over a second divorce. Both of his wives had had affairs. He was hurt and confused. He now had three children whom he loved deeply.*

Much to his credit, rather than remaining in bitterness and victimization, he explained, "I finally had to take a look at myself."

He was highly competitive and rising in a large corporation where the rules of promotion were stringent and unforgiving. There were no eight-hour workdays for those who wanted to excel. He'd started out both marriages wanting to find emotional connection, something he'd never felt in his childhood. But he didn't know how to truly open up, and although both relationships had looked solid from the outside, he'd remained a virtual stranger to both wives. Eventually, they found other, more emotionally supportive relationships.

Chase knew what was wrong but didn't know how to fix it. And the last thing he wanted for his children was to continue the pattern he'd created.

He began the intense work of combing through the emotional poverty of his childhood. It was only then that he realized how much shame had been a factor in his life. He'd been told by his father that he'd never be anything special, and the rule he was living by was that he would prove his father wrong—at any and all costs. Looking at his own son, he couldn't imagine saying such a thing to him. He began seeing that his frequent use of sarcasm and overly quick temper were present-day defensive reactions, triggered by childhood fears of abandonment and rejection. He allowed himself to feel, perhaps for the first time, what was in the moment.

He left therapy with a new sense of direction. He wanted these changes not only in his personal life but in his career as well. It was a risk. Would he lose his competitive edge if he developed a different style? Would he lose his team's respect? Despite his discomfort, he began talking to his immediate supervisor about wanting to become a better leader. Before, he'd been known to be quite tough on his team as he sought promotion after promotion. Now, he took trainings in how to guide others in building their own potential and how to adopt a forum for team feedback in the decision-making process.

*Chase's transformation made incredible changes in his parenting, as he admitted mistakes to his kids, came home earlier, and talked with them about their own struggles. And he smiled as he told me, "Where I was most amazed was at work. I'd had the fear that by being more open, I'd lose control. I'd be seen as indecisive or wishy-washy. Now people are asking to be on my team. And I'm getting feedback about how appreciated others feel, and thus their own productivity has increased immensely."*

Chase took his own sense of failure and turned it into positive change by letting go of perfectionism and following the five stages of healing. His journey took time and patience. But it brought him a new version of success, whereby his desire to change began affecting everything in his life.

## Now Your Work Continues

We've come to the final words of this book, and it's where your work continues in earnest. If you've moved in a direction that's rewarding to you, then you've discovered the hope that we talked about in the very beginning of this book—hope through actual change for a more authentic, more connected, and happier life.

Practice will make this way of being your new normal.

Let's talk about one more hurdle. When someone is losing the battle with depression and cannot stay away from darker thoughts of self-harm, they can choose to go into residential treatment. There is often tremendous reticence and even fear of doing so. But they go, work very hard, and learn a new potential for living a more stable life. Then a realization emerges: going home and resuming normal life will be even more difficult than initially seeking treatment.

That's where the hardest work can be. And it's what's in front of you. There are so many pulls and tugs from the old way of doing or thinking or feeling that holding on to a very fresh perspective and behavior can be challenging. Sometimes you have to end relationships that are too damaging, and you may need to set completely new boundaries in the ones that remain. This involves a healthy reappraisal of what you need now to stay stable. It can lead to short-term loss but also to long-term, huge gains.

You're worth fighting for, not despite all your imperfections and vulnerabilities but because of them. You're worth loving, not because of what you can do but because of who you are. You're growing in true strength, not because you always seem in control but because you can connect with and accept all of your emotions and allow them to guide you.

Thank you for giving me the honor of being part of your journey.

### Reflection 62: What Is My Dream?

Please use this final reflection to allow yourself to dream. What would your mantra for living be now? Where do you want to go? What can you imagine in your life that would bring you happiness? What kind of relationships do you want to grow in your own life? What do you want to learn that would bring you fulfillment? What do you want to discover in yourself and the world that would bring an inner smile of wonder? It's time for you to dream.

And know that whatever you choose to do, it won't be perfect. What it will be is a reflection of all of who you are.

# Acknowledgments

This book would never have existed without many people who offered their energy and guidance. First, let me introduce you to my friends and my team, each of whom appeared just when I needed them. The wise guidance of Jeannette Balleza Collins, who hit the "publish" button on my first blog post in 2012, has been incredible. A bit later came Christine Mathias, whose creative talent and enthusiasm have been an ongoing source of energy. When I met blogger and author Melissa Shultz, I had no idea she was an acquisitions editor for a literary agent. When she said, "I think my agent might want to look at this book on perfectly hidden depression," I was the luckiest writer in the world. That agent, Jim Donovan, and Melissa scoured over my first book proposal, whipping both me and it into professional shape, and introduced *Perfectly Hidden Depression* to potential publishers. I cannot thank them enough.

When acquiring editor Jennye Garibaldi contacted me that she would buy the book, not only did my heart sing, but I also jumped up and down like a schoolgirl finding out her braces were coming off. She could've asked me for anything at that moment, so I thank her for not. Both she and my developmental editor, Jennifer Holder, held my never-have-written-a-book hand and guided me to greater clarity of the vision and breadth of what I wanted to convey. Marisa Solís, my copy editor, painstakingly evaluated every sentence, questioning, deleting, asking for more explanation. And Karen Levy made revisions that tightened everything up and made it possible for even my Auntie Margaret (who was a grammar fanatic) to be proud. And, of course, a huge thank-you to New Harbinger, which took a risk on a new author and a fresh approach to talking about perfectionism and depression.

There's a group of people I'll never be able to thank publicly—and those are the hundreds of people who've emailed me after reading an article or listening to a podcast on perfectly hidden depression. They wrote, "I felt like you were describing me." "I've looked at depression criteria countless times and felt shame, afraid I was making up a problem." "You may have saved my life." Grieving parents who were totally confused about their happy, successful teenagers dying by suicide reached out to me and said, "I only wish I'd known this existed." These affirmations of the reality of what they've experienced motivated me like no other source. Even more thanks go to the more than fifty who shared not only their personal stories that you read here but also permission to use them.

And I can't forget not only my own patients but also so many others, who, via social media, have applauded my efforts. They've liked, commented, and cheered me on. My gratitude to you.

Jennifer Marshall graciously agreed to write a foreword for this book. She's one of the best examples I could imagine of someone using her own acceptance of her mental illness to transform not only her own life but also others' lives, and enrich our society by creating the nonprofit movement This Is My Brave.

I want to thank the Canadian perfectionism researchers and authors Dr. Gordon Flett and Dr. Paul Hewitt for personal interviews and support for *Perfectly Hidden Depression*. Dr. Michael Yapko also consulted with me on my ideas and was supportive of my endeavors.

I promised my friends almost two years ago when I began writing *Perfectly Hidden Depression* that I'd try very hard not to talk about the book constantly. I've likely failed in that attempt. But all of them continued to ask, "So, how's the book coming?" and their genuine caring has kept my head above water. The rest of the team I'm lucky enough to work with (Brenda Beatty, John Crowley, Rob Clinton, and Jodey Smith) have solved problems and kept the rest of my life afloat so I could focus on writing.

Everyone from my book club to my various school sidekicks, from fellow bloggers all over everywhere to Fayetteville folks, and even my workout buddies: all have kept the motivation coming. Bob Ford and Dr. David Joliffe—the only local authors I knew—met with me to offer guidance on the process. Great friends Keely Meyer, Kindra Richardson, Jonelle Lipscomb, Robert James, and Susan Gammon—what wonderful troopers you've all been to hang in there with me. My psychologist colleague and dear friend, Dr. Dina Hijazi, was always available to offer extremely sound clinical advice and her own unwavering belief in me. All gave much-needed reassurance for my own personal struggles, professional questions, and heightened vulnerability.

And then, there's my family. As I'm writing this, my oldest brother Adam is in hospice, having battled esophageal cancer and lost his fight. The grief is immense—for him, for us, and for the grandchildren he leaves behind. I am more than aware of his constant support, as well as that of Aunt Gay and my Dallas family, and the rest of my Arkansas family, my brother Spencer and his wife Debbie, Adam's wife Anne, and my nephews and their wives. My son Robinson's belief in me has been ever constant. When I said something one day about the growth I saw in him, his simple words were, "And I'm proud of yours as well." My last mention is definitely not the least—far from it. My husband, Richard, whom I adore, simply took over everything around the house. Everything, except for cooking. I might've lost a few pounds if that had been the case. He's listened. And listened. And listened.

I cannot think about the sorrow we all feel, as well as the simultaneous celebration of and gratitude for the gifts I've received from each and every one of my family members, without tears coming to my eyes.

I wish my mom and dad, who died more than a decade ago, were still alive. They both loved reading, and I think they would've been proud. I owe so much of my own sense of purpose and passion to them and am very thankful for the love we all shared, and still share, as a family. My mother, whose costly struggle with severe anxiety and perfectionism robbed her of a life of peace, said to me long ago, "If I'd known what I was doing to myself, I wouldn't have done it."

I can only hope my words help others like her.

# Resources

The National Suicide Prevention Lifeline is (800) 273-8255 in the United States. Most cities also have crisis hotlines that are available to you if needed.

I highly recommend all the books referenced in *Perfectly Hidden Depression*. As this is not a book on healing trauma or classic depression, I recommend the following titles to those who have suffered early childhood trauma or are looking for help with classic depression.

Bass, Ellen, and Laura Davis. 2008. *The Courage to Heal: A Guide for Women Survivors of Child Sexual Abuse.* New York: Harper-Collins.

Brown, Brené. 2012. *Daring Greatly: How the Courage to Be Vulnerable Transforms the Way We Live, Love, Parent, and Lead.* New York: Avery.

Lee, Mike. 2013. *Victims No Longer: The Classic Guide for Men Recovering from Sexual Child Abuse.* New York: Small Wonder Books.

Lerner, Harriet. 2014. *The Dance of Anger: A Woman's Guide to Changing the Patterns of Intimate Relationships.* New York: William Morrow.

Levine, Peter. 1997. *Waking the Tiger: Healing Trauma.* Berkeley, CA: North Atlantic Books.

Walker, Pete. 2013. *Complex PTSD: From Surviving to Thriving: A Guide and Map for Recovering from Childhood Trauma.* CreateSpace Independent Publishing Platform.

Yapko, Michael. 2001. *Treating Depression with Hypnosis.* New York: Yapko Publications.

# References

American Psychiatric Association. 2013. *The Diagnostic and Statistical Manual of Mental Disorders.* 5th ed. Washington, DC: American Psychiatric Publishing.

Angelou, M. 1993. *Wouldn't Take Nothing for My Journey Now.* New York: Bantam Books.

Barr, J. 2016. "Dear Class of 2020: Don't Let the Penn Face Get to You." *The Tab.* Penn State.

Batchelor, S. 1997. *Buddhism Without Belief.* New York: Riverhead Books.

Beaton, C. 2017. "Millennial Duck Syndrome: The Faked-Success Cycle That Hurts Everyone." *Psychology Today*, May 20.

Blatt, S. 1995. "The Destructiveness of Perfectionism: Implications for the Treatment of Depression." *American Psychologist* 50(12): 1,003–1,020.

Burns, David. 1999. *The Feeling Good Handbook.* New York: Plume.

Carson, Rick. 2003. *Taming Your Gremlin: A Surprisingly Simple Method for Getting Out of Your Own Way.* New York: Quill.

Brown, B. 2010. *The Gifts of Imperfection.* Center City, MN: Hazelden Publishing.

Curtin, S., M. Warner, and H. Hedegaard. 2016. "Increase in Suicide in the United States, 1999-2014." NCHS data brief, no. 241. April. Hyattsville, MD: National Center for Health Statistics.

Fagan, K. 2017. *What Made Maddy Run.* New York: Little, Brown and Company.

Flamenbaum, R., and R. R. Holden. 2007. "Psychache as a Mediator in the Relationship Between Perfectionism and Suicidality." *Journal of Counseling Psychology* 54(1): 51–61.

Flett, G., P. Hewitt, and S. Mikail. 2017. *Perfectionism: A Relational Approach to Conceptualization, Assessment, and Treatment.* New York: The Guilford Press.

Harris, D. 2014. *10% Happier: How I Tamed the Voice in My Head, Reduced Stress Without Losing My Edge, and Found Self-Help That Actually Works—A True Story.* New York: HarperCollins.

Johnson, S. 2011. *Who Moved My Cheese?* New York: G. P. Putnam's Sons.

Kabat-Zinn, J. 1994. *Wherever You Go, There You Are.* New York: Hyperion.

Kubler-Ross, E. 2014. *On Death and Dying.* New York: Scribner.

Lamott, A. 1995. *Bird by Bird.* New York: Anchor.

Lawson, C. A. 2000. *Understanding the Borderline Mother: Helping Her Children Transcend the Intense, Unpredictable and Volatile Relationship.* New York: Rowman & Littlefield.

Lawson, J. 2015. *Furiously Happy: A Funny Book About Horrible Things.* New York: Flatiron Books.

National Institute of Mental Health. 2018. "Suicide." Last updated May 2018. https://www.nimh.nih.gov/health/statistics/suicide .shtml.

National Institute of Mental Health. 2019a. "Major Depression." Last updated February 2019. https://www.nimh.nih.gov/health /statistics/major-depression.shtml.

National Institute of Mental Health. 2019b. "Mental Illness." Last updated February 2019. https://www.nimh.nih.gov/health/statis tics/mental-illness.shtml.

Neff, K. 2014. *Self-Compassion: The Proven Power of Being Kind to Yourself.* New York: William Morrow.

Pacht, A. R. 1984. "Reflections on Perfection." *American Psychologist* 39(4): 386–390.

Real, T. 1997. *I Don't Want to Talk About It.* New York: Scribner.

Ruiz, D. M. 1997. *The Four Agreements.* San Rafael, CA: Amber-Allen Publishing.

Shneidman, E. 1993. *Suicide as Psychache: A Clinical Approach to Self-Destructive Behavior.* Northvale, NJ: Aronson.

Siegel, D. 2018. *Aware: The Science and Practice of Presence.* New York: Penguin Random House.

Solomon, A. 2001. *The Noonday Demon: An Atlas of Depression.* New York: Scribner.

Twenge, J. 2017. *iGen: Why Today's Super-Connected Kids Are Growing Up Less Rebellious, More Tolerant, Less Happy—and Completely Unprepared for Adulthood.* New York: Atria Books.

Van der Kolk, B. 2014. *The Body Keeps the Score.* New York: Penguin Books.

Vendel, C. 2018. "University Ignored Daughter's Suicidal Pleas, Parents Say in Lawsuit." *Penn Live,* April 10.

Williams, M., J. Teasdale, J. Z. Segal, and J. Kabat-Zinn. 2007. *The Mindful Way through Depression: Freeing Yourself from Chronic Unhappiness.* New York: The Guilford Press.

Wilson, R. 2009. *Don't Panic.* New York: Harper Collins.

Winfrey, O. 2017. *The Wisdom of Sundays: Life-Changing Insights from Super Soul Conversations.* New York: Flatiron Books.

Yapko, M. 1998. *Breaking the Patterns of Depression.* New York: Broadway Books.

**Margaret Robinson Rutherford, PhD,** is a clinical psychologist in private practice with more than twenty-five years of experience treating individuals and couples for depression, anxiety, and relationship issues. She also offers her compassionate and commonsense therapeutic style to the general public through her popular blog and podcasts, with the goal of decreasing the stigma around psychological treatment. Her podcasts and shows on perfectly hidden depression (PHD) have reached thousands, as she sheds light on this overlooked presentation of the disease.

Foreword writer **Jennifer Marshall** is cofounder of This Is My Brave, a national storytelling series dedicated to discussing mental illness. Jennifer was diagnosed with bipolar I disorder in 2006 at the age of twenty-six, and writing about her life with a mental illness has helped her healing process. You can read her blog, *Bipolar Mom Life*, or follow her on Twitter: @BipolarMomLife.

# MORE BOOKS *from*
# NEW HARBINGER PUBLICATIONS

**THE CBT WORKBOOK
FOR PERFECTIONISM**

Evidence-Based Skills to Help
You Let Go of Self-Criticism,
Build Self-Esteem & Find Balance

**978-1684031535 / US $24.95**

**WHEN PERFECT ISN'T
GOOD ENOUGH,
SECOND EDITION**

Strategies for Coping
with Perfectionism

**978-1572245594 / US $19.95**

**THE UPWARD SPIRAL**

Using Neuroscience to Reverse
the Course of Depression,
One Small Change at a Time

**978-1626251205 / US $17.95**

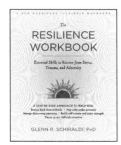

**THE RESILIENCE
WORKBOOK**

Essential Skills to Recover from
Stress, Trauma & Adversity

**978-1626259409 / US $24.95**

**ANXIETY HAPPENS**

52 Ways to Find Peace of Mind

**978-1684031108 / US $14.95**

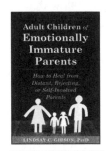

**ADULT CHILDREN
OF EMOTIONALLY
IMMATURE PARENTS**

How to Heal from Distant,
Rejecting, or Self-Involved Parents

**978-1626251700 / US $17.95**